DK EYEWITNESS

T0024044

TOP **10**
DUBLIN

Top 10 Dublin Highlights

The Top 10 of Everything

CONTENTS

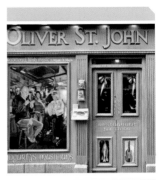

Dublin and Ireland Area by Area

Streetsmart

The rapid rate at which the world is changing is constantly keeping the DK Eyewitness team on our toes. While we've worked hard to ensure that this edition of Dublin is accurate and up-to-date, we know that opening hours alter, standards shift, prices fluctuate, places close and new ones pop up in their stead. So, if you notice we've got something wrong or left something out, we want to hear about it. Please get in touch at **travelguides@dk.com**

Within each Top 10 list in this book, no hierarchy of quality or popularity is implied. All 10 are, in the editor's opinion, of roughly equal merit.

Title page, front cover and spine
Ha'penny Bridge at dusk
Back cover, clockwise from top left
Guinness Storehouse; Phoenix Park; Grafton Street; Ha'penny Bridge; Trinity College

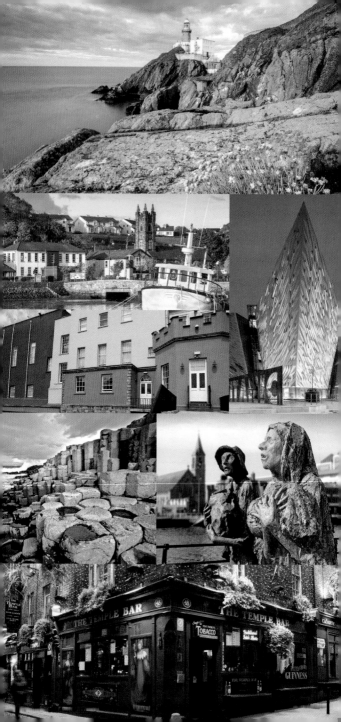

Welcome to
Dublin

The word "craic" sums up the spirit of Dublin. Just like the city, it represents a bubbling, sparky mix of fun and banter, warmth and conviviality. This is quite possibly the most sociable city in the world. With DK Eyewitness Top 10 Dublin, it's yours to explore.

Dublin is a place that loves to party, as any evening spent on the cobblestones of the busy **Temple Bar** district will prove. But Ireland's capital has much more to offer than just its famous pubs. It has gorgeous **Georgian architecture** and a number of world-class **museums** and **galleries**, many of them free to visit, and some of them gathered around the picturesque quadrangles of ancient **Trinity College**.

Beyond the metropolis, Ireland is a nation rich in myths and legends, with irresistible coastal scenery running all the way from **Kerry** to **Donegal**, and a burgeoning food culture in cities such as **Kilkenny** and **Cork**. Move inland, and you'll find the heartlands of Ireland: megalithic sites stand in the shadows of rolling green hills and hundreds of lakes hold tiny picturesque islands. Beyond the bigger, well-known cities, there are peaceful counties and villages where you may well be the only tourist in sight. Think seaside hamlets in **Donegal**, or remote Gaeltacht (Irish speaking) communities in **Mayo**.

Whether you're coming for a weekend or a week, our Top 10 guide brings together the best of everything that the city and country have to offer, from atmospheric monastic ruins and fine art to a peerless pint of Guinness or plate of prawns or oysters. The guide has useful tips throughout, from seeking out what's free to places off the beaten path, plus five easy-to-follow itineraries designed to tie together a clutch of sights in a short space of time. Add inspiring photography and detailed maps, and you've got the essential pocket-sized travel companion. **Enjoy the book, and enjoy Dublin.**

Clockwise from top: The headland at Howth, Titanic Belfast, the Famine Memorial in Dublin, Temple Bar pub, the Giant's Causeway, colourful buildings in Dublin Castle grounds, Bantry Bay

Exploring Dublin

Dublin is a place to take your time over: linger over a pint, share a story, watch the River Liffey glide by. But if your time is limited, here's how to grab the city's highlights in a whistle-stop weekend, along with a fun and action-packed, week-long driving tour taking in the best of Ireland.

The **Guinness Storehouse** is the best place to learn all about Ireland's national drink.

Key
— Two-day itinerary
— Seven-day itinerary

GALWAY
Galway
CLARE
LIMERICK
7
KERRY
Dingle Peninsula
The Chart House Restaurant
6
Killarney National Park
Cork
5
Ring of Kerry
Kenmare
CORK
Kinsale

Two Days in Dublin

Day ❶
MORNING
From College Green, wander through the courtyards of **Trinity College** (see pp12–13), dropping inside to marvel at the Book of Kells. Next head for the **National Museum** (see pp14–15), choosing between Viking skeletons in the Archaeology Museum and the Dead Zoo at the Natural History Museum. Stop for lunch at the museum's café.

AFTERNOON
Swerve into grassy **St Stephen's Green** (see p61) for a pondside walk, then window-shop your way along Grafton Street en route to **Temple Bar** (see pp22–3), which buzzes with attractions. Project Arts Centre and the Irish Film Institute have entertainment options for later, or you can just hit the bars. If the madness gets too much, nearby **Christ Church Cathedral** (see pp24–5) offers a quiet spot for some contemplation.

Day ❷
MORNING
Start with a sobering circuit of **Kilmainham Gaol** (see pp32–3): it pays to pre-book; the first tour is at 9:30am daily. Then stroll the tree-lined avenue to Royal Hospital Kilmainham, for cutting-edge art at IMMA. Its basement café is great for lunch.

AFTERNOON
It's a shortish walk to the **Guinness Storehouse** (see pp30–31). Here, enjoy a panoramic pint in the Gravity Bar before returning to downtown Dublin, perhaps via the **Brazen Head**

[see p51], Dublin's oldest pub. If you've time, explore **Dublin Castle** [see pp18–19], home to a pretty garden and the free Chester Beatty [see pp20–21].

Seven Days in Ireland

Day ❶ and ❷
Follow the two-day Dublin itinerary.

Day ❸
WICKLOW MOUNTAINS
For a hit of wild hills, head south into County Wicklow, spending a morning at fountain-sprinkled **Powerscourt Estate** [see p75], then on to striking **Glendalough** [see p84], for enigmatic monastic ruins and a lovely walk by the lakeside. Overnight in **Kilkenny** [see p88], with its brace of Michelin-starred restaurants.

Day ❹
CORK
Ireland's second city [see p95] has a truly continental air, with a

lip-smacking food scene and splendid music and ballet at the Opera House [see p96]. For a less frenetic itinerary, skip Galway and add a day at nearby **Kinsale** [see p96], treating yourself to super-fresh shell-fish on the multicoloured seafront.

Day ❺
KILLARNEY
Forty square miles of lakes, mountains and marauding red deer await in Killarney National Park – the way to see it all is by taking a jaunt in a car, or a traditional pony-and-trap [see p91]. Nearby **Kenmare** [see p92] has good options for dinner and digs.

Day ❻
DINGLE PENINSULA
The Ring of Kerry has endless dramatic driving, and a loop around the Dingle Peninsula gives a great flavour, taking in ocean views, early Christian relics and lunch at Dingle's **The Chart House Restaurant** [see p93].

Day ❼
GALWAY CITY
The cobbled city of **Galway** [see p105] is full of live music and bustling pubs – it even has its own Latin Quarter.

Visitors sitting outside Quays Bar in **Galway City**.

Top 10 Dublin Highlights

The magnificent Long Room at
Trinity College's Old Library, Dublin

🔟 Dublin Highlights

One of the most visited capitals in Europe, Dublin is a city steeped in history. Huddled together within a compact area are Viking remains, medieval cathedrals and churches, Georgian squares and world-class museums. But it's not just about buildings and artifacts – music, theatre, literature and pubs play just as strong a part in Dublin's make-up and atmosphere.

Trinity College ①

The elder statesman of Ireland's universities, Trinity is also one of the oldest in Europe. Its buildings and grounds are a landmark in the heart of the city (see pp12–13).

② National Museum of Ireland

This museum is housed across three locations, each specializing in a particular area of science, history and culture (see pp14–15).

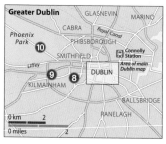

Greater Dublin

National Gallery of Ireland ③

Wonderful Italian, French, Dutch and Spanish works are exhibited here, alongside a great collection of Irish art (see pp16–17).

④ Dublin Castle

The castle was built into the city's medieval walls and protected by the River Liffey to the north and in the south and east by the now underground River Poddle (see pp18–21).

5 Temple Bar
This historic part of the city has been revamped into one of its busiest areas. There is no shortage of places to eat and drink *(see pp22–3)*.

6 Christ Church Cathedral
Gothic, Romanesque and Victorian features jostle for attention in this former Viking church *(see pp24–5)*.

7 St Patrick's Cathedral
Known colloquially as the "People's Cathedral", this is one of the earliest Christian sites in the city. It is also the burial ground for Jonathan Swift, author of *Gulliver's Travels (see pp28–9)*.

O'Connell Bridge
Butt Bridge
GEORGE'S QUAY
DOYLE STREET
TARA ST
TOWNSEND STREET
PEARSE STREET
1
NASSAU ST
WESTLAND ROW
LEINSTER ST SOUTH
DAWSON ST
KILDARE STREET
3
Merrion Square
2
STEPHEN'S GREEN NORTH
phen's een

0 metres 400
0 yards 400

8 Guinness Storehouse
A pint of Guinness could be the country's national symbol. This exhibition at the Guinness Brewery ends with a free pint of the black stuff *(see pp30–31)*.

9 Kilmainham Gaol and Hospital
After a sobering tour of the one-time prison, lighten the mood at the former hospital, which now houses the Irish Museum of Modern Art *(see pp32–3)*.

10 Phoenix Park
This is one of the largest city parks in Europe. Historic monuments and Dublin Zoo are only two of its delights *(see pp34–5)*.

🔟 ⭐ Trinity College

Trinity College is Dublin's most famous educational institution and, since its foundation in the 16th century, has produced many impressive alumni, including Jonathan Swift, Sally Rooney, Mary Robinson, Oscar Wilde, Bram Stoker and Samuel Beckett. Entering through the college's West Front is like walking into a bucolic time-warp: a cobbled quadrangle, smooth green lawns and an array of fine 18th- and 19th-century buildings. A number of the buildings are open to the public, one of them being the Printing House, home to one of the country's greatest treasures, the *Book of Kells*.

NEED TO KNOW

MAP F4 ■ College Green, Dublin 2 ■ 01 896 1000 ■ www.tcd.ie

Open May–Sep: 8:30am–5pm Mon–Sat, 9:30am–5pm Sun; Oct–Apr: 9:30am–5pm Mon–Sat, noon–4:30pm Sun (library)

Book of Kells: adm €18.50

■ In South Frederick Street a very good Italian delicatessen, Dunne & Crescenzi, serves delicious snacks and meals.

■ In autumn 2023, the Old Library will close for a three-year preservation project. During this time, the *Book of Kells* will be displayed in the Printing House.

1 Front Arch

College Green, facing the Front Arch entrance to Trinity, was originally called Hoggen Green. The statues of Edmund Burke and Oliver Goldsmith flanking the entrance were made by sculptor John Foley.

2 Douglas Hyde Gallery

One of Ireland's leading contemporary art galleries, the Douglas Hyde has exhibitions by both emerging and well-established artists.

3 Chapel

The chapel is the only one in Ireland shared by all Christian denominations. The stained-glass window above the altar dates from 1871.

4 Old Library

Built between 1712 and 1732, Trinity's Old Library (below) is one of Dublin's most recognizable landmarks. The finest feature is the 64-m (200-ft) Long Room, with two tiers of antiquated oak bookcases holding more than 200,000 books.

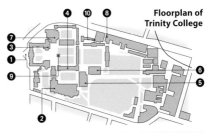

Floorplan of Trinity College

5 Berkeley Library Building

In front of Paul Koralek's 1967 creation is the sculpture **(above)** *Sphere within a Sphere* (1982) by Arnaldo Pomodoro.

THE HISTORY OF TRINITY COLLEGE

Founded in 1592 by Queen Elizabeth I on the site of All Hallows Monastery, Trinity College's aim was to provide young Protestants with an alternative to European universities where they might fall under the influence of Catholicism. The Anglican bias lasted into the 1970s.

Students in the quadrangle, Trinity College

6 Museum Building

This fine Venetian-style edifice was completed in 1857. A pair of giant Irish deer skeletons stand guard in the magnificent hall. There are no museums here today, but Trinity's zoological collection is open to the public in summer – find it in the Zoology Building, nearby.

10 Printing House

The *Book of Kells* **(left)** will temporarily be on display in the Printing House, alongside a new exhibition. One of the city's most treasured possessions, this illustrated manuscript is thought to date from 800 CE. The building itself is an impressive, pillared structure built in 1734.

7 Dining Hall

Trinity's many students eat at this grand dining hall which was originally built by Richard Cassels in 1742. However, it has been considerably altered over the past 250 years and restored after a fire in 1984.

9 Campanile

Designed by Sir Charles Lanyon, the architect of Queen's University in Belfast, this 30-m- (100-ft-) bell tower **(right)**, is the centrepiece of Trinity's main quad. It is enclosed by 18th- and 19th-century buildings.

8 Samuel Beckett Theatre

Opened in 1992, the Samuel Beckett Theatre showcases the work of the drama department and hosts prestigious Irish and international companies.

TOP 10 ⭐ National Museum of Ireland

There are three different branches of this outstanding museum. The Kildare Street location features the Archaeology Museum, which traces the history of Ireland, including the country's prehistoric early culture. The Merrion Street branch comprises the Natural History Museum. The third branch out at Collins Barracks is the Decorative Arts and History Museum. It offers a unique experience with the most up-to-date display techniques portraying the country's decorative arts and social, military, economic and political history.

1 Façade
The exterior of the museum in Kildare Street (above) is an example of Victorian Palladian style. The rotunda is modelled on the Pantheon in Rome.

3 Treasury
Part of a hoard found in County Limerick in 1808, the Ardagh Chalice (below) is probably the Archaeology Museum's most famous object. The mid-8th-century chalice is a beautiful example of the Irish Early Christian metalworker's craft. Another beauty from this collection is the Tara Brooch.

NEED TO KNOW

Archaeology Museum:
MAP F5; Kildare St, Dublin 2; 01 677 7444; **Open** 10am–5pm Tue–Sat, 1–5pm Sun & Mon; www.museum.ie

Natural History Museum:
MAP G5; Merrion St, Dublin 2

Decorative Arts and History Museum, Collins Barracks:
MAP A3; Benburb St, Dublin 7

■ There's a good café at Collins Barracks.

■ The gift shop in Kildare Street has jewellery made by local designers to reflect the museum's collection.

2 Proclaiming a Republic: The 1916 Rising
Events surrounding Easter Week in 1916 *(see p39)* are vividly portrayed through stories and objects in Collins Barracks. Exhibits include the Irish Republic flag which was hoisted over the General Post Office.

4 What's In Store
At the Collins Barracks branch, this exhibition is one of the highlights of the Decorative Arts and History Museum *(see p72)*, which features a visible storage display. More than 16,000 objects (left) from the decorative arts collection are accessible to the public in one space.

MUSEUM GUIDE
To visit all three parts of the city's National Museum on the same day, start with the Natural History Museum in Merrion Square. From here the Archaeology Museum is only a short walk: turn right at the lights on Merrion Row, head along the north side of St Stephen's Green, then turn right onto Kildare Street. The easiest way to get from here to the third and last wing, Collins Barracks, is to take the handy tourist "Do Dublin" Hop-on Hop-off bus (www.do dublin.ie) over to the north side of the river.

⑤ Soldiers and Chiefs

Explore over 1,000 military artifacts, such as swords, uniforms, letters and firearms at this Decorative Arts and History exhibition (see p72). It also includes the fascinating Stokes Tapestry **(above)**, depicting battle scenes from Irish history.

⑥ Irish Silver

The silver collection at the Decorative Arts and History Museum (see p72) shows a huge variety of styles. The arrival of French Huguenot silversmiths in Dublin had a strong influence on local design.

⑦ Viking Ireland

This exhibition in the Archaeology Museum explores Ireland's Viking Age – which extended from 800 CE to 1150 – through objects found at a number of Viking graves and sites in and around Dublin.

⑧ Prehistoric Ireland

Sight the unique Lurgan Longboat, made from hollowed-out oak trunks, dating from around 2500 BCE at the Archaeology Museum. Other exhibits include the cast bronze horns, probably played like the Australian didgeridoo.

⑨ Ór – Ireland's Gold

Displayed at the Archaeology Museum, this superb collection of ancient gold objects **(below)** was found in counties as far apart as County Clare and County Derry. The pieces show great skill and invention.

⑩ Fonthill Vase

This bluish-white vase is the only surviving example of porcelain to have left China in the 14th century and whose history can be traced from that moment on. Displayed at Decorative Arts and History (see p72).

TOP 10 ★ National Gallery of Ireland

The National Gallery's outstanding collection of Western European art ranges from the Middle Ages to the mid-20th century and includes the most important gathering of Irish art in the world. This purpose-built gallery was opened to the public in January 1864, initially displaying a collection of just 112 pictures. The Milltown Wing was added in 1903, the Beit Wing in 1968 and the Millennium Wing in 2002. The gallery has benefited from some important donors during its history, including Countess Milltown, George Bernard Shaw, Sir Hugh Lane, Chester Beatty and Sir Alfred and Lady Beit. Its collection has grown to over 16,300 artworks, comprising paintings, prints and sculptures.

1 The Liffey Swim
The gallery's Yeats Archive includes an impressive collection of Jack Butler Yeats' paintings, ranging from this early favourite, *The Liffey Swim* **(below)**, from 1923, to later expressionistic work such as *Grief* from 1951.

2 The Taking of Christ
Caravaggio's moving 1602 work is the highlight of the gallery's display of Baroque paintings, which also takes in Orazio Gentileschi and Rutilio Manetti. Other Italian painters featured include Uccello, Titian, Tintoretto and Canaletto.

3 Amorino
The precocious Antonio Canova was the most gifted and innovative sculptor of the late 18th and early 19th centuries. This marble, *Amorino*, was commissioned in 1789 by John La Touche, the son of Ireland's richest banker.

⑤ Argenteuil Basin with a Single Sailboat

Claude Monet's 1874 painting **(above)** is a highlight in the gallery's very fine collection of 17th- to 19th-century French art.

⑥ Kitchen Maid with the Supper at Emmaus

This early work by Diego Velázquez is part of a Spanish collection spanning five centuries. Other Spanish works include five canvases by Goya, including *Portrait of Doña Antonia Zárate*.

⑦ The Cottage Girl

The ragged "cottage girl" **(below)** is one of Thomas Gainsborough's most famous "fancy pictures".

④ Christ in the House of Martha and Mary

This painting **(above)**, is an interesting collaborative work which was painted in 1628. The painting features landscape by Jan Brueghel the Younger and figures by Peter Paul Rubens.

⑧ Still Life with a Mandolin

Strikingly vibrant the *Still Life with a Mandolin* is from Pablo Picasso's time in Juan-les-Pins, on the Côte d'Azur, in 1924. Here he had worked on large-scale Cubist still-lifes, which are imbued with the exuberant light and colours of the sunny Mediterranean.

⑨ Pastures at Malahide

Painted by Nathaniel Hone, the Younger, this painting (1894–96) is part of a strong showing by Irish Impressionists. Hone travelled to Paris and the artists' colonies at Brittany and Barbizon.

⑩ Self-Portrait as Timanthes

A fine collection of Irish art includes *Self-Portrait as Timanthes*, by 18th-century Neo-Classical painter James Barry, whose work influenced William Blake.

📟🔟 ⭐ Dublin Castle

The imposing structure of Dublin Castle was a controversial symbol of British rule for 700 years, until it was formally handed over to Michael Collins and the Irish Free State in 1922. Commissioned by King John in the 13th century, the castle evolved from a medieval fortress into a vice-regal court and administrative centre. It has suffered numerous tribulations in its history, but the most concerted attack was in 1534, when it was besieged by "Silken Thomas" Fitzgerald (so called for his finely embroidered robes), who had renounced his allegiance to the English Crown. Its current use is primarily ceremonial. Visitors can tour the ornate state apartments and explore the courtyards and museums.

BUILDING DUBLIN CASTLE

In 1204, 30 years after the Anglo-Norman landed in Ireland, King John ordered a castle to be built in Dublin. Much of this medieval castle was destroyed by a fire in 1684 and Sir William Robinson completed the new apartments by 1688. Most of these were replaced in the 18th century.

② Figure of Justice

Guarding the main entrance is the Figure of Justice. It faces the Upper Yard, turning its back on the city – as some cynically commented, an apt symbol of British justice.

③ Bermingham Tower Room

This former medieval prison was converted into a state apartment.

④ The Throne Room

The throne (above) is flanked by roundels and ovals depicting Minerva, Jupiter, Juno and Mars. This was the most important ceremonial space in the state apartments.

① The Chester Beatty and Gallery

A stunning collection *(see pp20–21)* of artistic, religious and secular works from around the world dating from 2700 BCE to the present.

⑤ The Bedford Tower

In 1907, the Irish "Crown Jewels" – a diamond St Patrick Star and Badge – were stolen from here and never recovered.

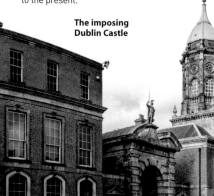

The imposing Dublin Castle

NEED TO KNOW

MAP D4 ■ Dame Street, Dublin 2

Castle: 01 645 8813; open 9:45am–5:45pm daily (last adm 5:15pm); adm €8 (€12 guided tour); www.dublincastle.ie

Chester Beatty: 01 407 0750; open Mar–Oct: 9:45am–5:30pm Mon, Tue & Thu–Sat (until 8pm Wed), noon–5:30pm Sun; Nov–Feb: closed Mon; www.chester beatty.ie

■ Try the Silk Road Café *(see p63)* on the ground floor of the Chester Beatty.

6 Gardens

To the back of the chapel are the Dubh Linn Gardens **(above)**, located on the site of the "Black Pool" harbour from which the city gets its name.

7 The Chapel Royal

The exterior of this fine Gothic revival building is decorated with 103 sculpted heads, beautifully carved out of Tullamore limestone.

9 The State Apartments

The state apartments feature an exceptional collection of paintings by the Old Masters. There are over 150 works on permanent display here.

St Patrick's Hall 8

Dedicated to Ireland's patron saint, the hall **(right)** has the ceiling painted by Waldré (1742–1814) depicting incidents in British and Irish history, such as St Patrick lighting the Pascal Fire on the Hill of Slane.

Floorplan of Dublin Castle

10 Viking Undercroft

Excavations show the remains of the original castle, including part of a 10th-century town and the moat.

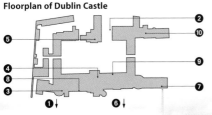

Chester Beatty Guide

Japanese picture book

manuscripts produced under the guidance of the Mughal emperors Akbar, Shah Jahan and Jahangir.

① Japanese Picture Books

Some of the finest pieces in the Japanese collection are the illustrated handscrolls and albums of a type known as *Nara Ehon* (Nara picture books).

② Bust of Chester Beatty

A bust of Alfred Chester Beatty by the sculptor Carolyn Mulholland is on display in the atrium.

③ Mughal-era Indian Collection

This collection includes some of the best paintings and illustrated

A painting from the Mughal era

④ Illuminated Manuscripts

Exceptional illuminated manuscripts can be found throughout the library. The illustration "Bahram Gur Slays a Dragon", from the *Book of Kings (Shahnama)* by Firdausi, was made in Iran during the Ilkhanid period (1300) and is one of the finest.

Japanese woodblock print

⑤ Woodblocks

The *ukiyo-e* woodblock prints complement the outstanding set of more than 700 prints known as *surimono*. These prints, like modern-day greetings cards, were created to mark special events or occasions.

⑥ Papyrus Texts

Papyrus is an aquatic plant from which ancient Egyptians made writing materials for their documents. One of the finest here is Paul's Letter to the Romans (around 180–200 CE). The hiero-glyphic and demotic papyri relate to administrative and burial practices.

⑦ Japanese Inrō

These tiny, intricately decorated boxes were used to store seals and medicines and are repro-duced today by some perfumiers.

8 Chinese Collection

An eclectic display from the Qing dynasty includes snuff bottles, jade books and a stunning range of silk dragon robes.

9 The Qur'an Collection

This gathering of more than 250 Qur'ans and Qur'an fragments is considered to be the most important of its kind outside the Middle East. Ibn al-Bawwab

Silk dragon robe, Chinese Collection

is reputed to be one of the greatest medieval Islamic calligraphers and displayed here is the exquisite Qur'an he copied in Baghdad in 1001.

10 The Persian Poets

For connoisseurs of Persian poetry, famed Firdawsi, Nizami, Hafiz and Jami are just four of the authors that feature in the 330 manuscripts in this collection.

ALFRED CHESTER BEATTY

Alfred Chester Beatty was born in New York in 1875, and spent much of his childhood collecting stamps, minerals and Chinese snuff bottles. In adulthood, running a highly successful mining consultancy, he could afford to pursue his interests and gathered together this outstanding collection of Islamic manuscripts, Chinese, Japanese and other Asian Art. Beatty lived and worked in both New York and London before finally deciding to settle in Dublin in 1950. The first library for his collection was built on Shrewsbury Road, and was relocated to Dublin Castle in 2000. Beatty loved Ireland and contributed generously to its galleries and cultural institutions. In 1957, he became the country's first honorary citizen, and decided to leave his library in trust for the benefit of the public. He died in 1968 and was accorded a state funeral – a first for someone born outside Ireland.

TOP 10 ARTIFACTS

1 Paul's Letter to the Romans c.180–200 CE (Western collection)

2 Illuminations of the *Walsingham Bible* c.1153 (Western collection)

3 Egyptian love poems, 1160 BCE (Western collection)

4 *Scenes from a Noh Play*, 17th century (East Asian collection)

5 *Qur'an*, copied by Ibn al-Bawwab, 1001 (Islamic collection)

6 *The Tale of Oriole*, late 17th century (East Asian collection)

7 Luke 6: 30-41, Four Gospels and the Acts of the Apostles, 200–250 CE (Western collection)

8 *The Madonna on a Grassy Bank*, Dürer, 1503 (Western collection)

9 Jade snuff bottle, c.1750–1800 (East Asian collection)

10 The Roleau Vase, early 18th century (East Asian collection)

(Displays change often; see website or call ahead)

Rare, illuminated Western manuscripts

TOP 10 ⭐ Temple Bar

A lively enclave of cafés, bars and theatres, the Temple Bar area covers the cobbled streets that stretch between Dame Street and the River Liffey, and from Fishamble Street to Westmoreland Street. Known as Dublin's cultural quarter, Temple Bar always has something going on, especially in summer and autumn. Summer brings outdoor film screenings, street theatre and live music, while autumn sees the Dublin Theatre Festival, Culture Night and Fringe Festival.

1 City Hall

Built by Thomas Cooley in 1769–79, the building **(below)** was originally the Royal Exchange, but became the City Hall *(see p63)* in the mid-19th century. Built of Portland stone, it is a fine example of Neo-Classical style.

A lively pedestrianized cobbled street in Temple Bar

2 Merchant's Arch

A formal entry point to the area, the arch dates from the days when ships sailed right up the Liffey to dock and trade.

3 Meeting House Square

Named after a Quaker Meeting Hall, this is the centre of Temple Bar. It is the venue for concerts, plays **(below)** and the Saturday food market. In the summer, movies are screened under the giant canopy.

4 Irish Rock 'n' Roll Museum Experience

Set around gig venue the Button Factory and the iconic Temple Lane Studios, this interactive museum reminisces the history of popular Irish music.

5 Cow's Lane

This pedestrian street has designer boutiques and chic coffee bars. Fashion and gift stalls line the centre path at the Designer Mart on Saturdays from spring to late autumn.

Map of Temple Bar

(see p48)

6 Project Arts Centre

This modern arts centre (see p48), was established in 1966 as a three-week festival. Today it is known for avant-garde theatre, dance, music and film.

7 Millennium Bridge

One of the pedestrian-only bridges that cross the Liffey, the Millennium Bridge's simple lines perfectly complement its more famous and more ornate companion, the Ha'penny Bridge (see p64). The bridge links the shopping areas north and south of the Liffey.

8 Photo Museum Ireland

This contemporary space (see p64) hosts exhibitions by Irish and international photographers. It offers photography courses and dark rooms for rent.

9 Irish Film Institute

One of the first major cultural projects in Temple Bar, the Irish Film Institute houses the offices of independent film organizations and a lively café. It also features three screens.

REGENERATION

Sir William Temple bought this land in the 1600s and reclaimed the marshland to bring trade to the centre. However, with the development of the docks to the east, business began to slowly decline. In the 1960s, traders made use of the cheap rent and the area took on a Bohemian air. In the 1990s the government regenerated the whole Temple Bar area.

10 The Ark

There's a magical mini-amphitheatre (see p47) and lots of bright spaces for getting crafty at Europe's first custom-built children's cultural centre **(below)**. Irish and international artists have developed the fun programmes, including exhibitions and theatre workshops.

🔟 ⭐ Christ Church Cathedral

The spectacularly imposing cathedral that we see today is largely a result of 19th-century restoration. Dublin's first church, made of wood, was founded here in 1030 by Sitric Silkenbeard, the first Christian king of the Dublin Norsemen. In 1172, however, Norman Richard de Clare, known as Strongbow, demolished the first church and commissioned his own stone version. During the Reformation, the cathedral passed to the Protestant Church and, along with St Patrick's Cathedral, it remains within the Church of Ireland.

1 Medieval Carvings

Decorating the columns at the entrance to the North Transept, these 12th-century carvings depict two human faces with griffons and musicians. The middle pillar of the nave is adorned with fine Gothic heads.

2 Crypt

The vast crypt, the city's oldest structure, is unusual in that it runs the entire length of the building (see p62). It houses the treasury exhibition and a mummified cat and rat.

3 Strongbow's Tomb

This tomb (below) of the Norman conqueror of Ireland is a 16th-century replica. The effigy is not thought to be Strongbow. However, it is possible that the fragment lying beside the tomb may be part of the original.

4 Great Nave

The 25-m- (80-ft-) high nave (above) raises the spirits with its fine early Gothic arches. On the north side, the 13th-century wall leans out by 50 cm (1.5 ft), a result of the collapse of the south wall in 1562.

5 Romanesque Doorway

This doorway, found on the southside entrance to the cathedral, is a fine example of 12th-century Irish stonework.

STRONGBOW

In the 12th century, the exiled king of Leinster, Dermot MacMurrough, looked to the Anglo-Normans for help to recover his kingdom. Richard de Clare, also known as Strongbow, answered the call and arrived with his knights. He routed Leinster and conquered Dublin, then affirmed his loyalty to Henry II. It began centuries of English hold over Irish land.

6 Bridge to Synod Hall

An ornate Gothic bridge (above) was added during the rebuilding of the cathedral in the 1870s. Synod Hall is home to Dublinia (see p62), a re-creation of ancient Dublin.

7 Chapel of St Laud

This chapel is named after the 5th-century Normandy Bishop of Coutances. The chapel used to hold the alleged heart of Dublin's 12th-century patron saint, Laurence O'Toole. The heart was stolen in 2012, but recovered in 2018.

8 Lady Chapel

One of the other chapels opening off the central choir area is used to celebrate the daily Eucharist and provides a more intimate setting than the nave of the cathedral when numbers are small.

9 Lord Mayor's Pew

Generally known as the Civic Pew, but historically associated with the Lord Mayor, it is kept in the north aisle, but is moved to the front of the nave when required for ceremonial use. It is decorated with a carving of the city. There is also a rest for the civic mace.

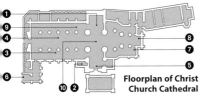

Floorplan of Christ Church Cathedral

10 Quire

At the centre of the church, the Victorian wooden stalls (above) are set out for the choir. The Archbishop's Throne is set in pride of place.

NEED TO KNOW

Christ Church Cathedral: **MAP D4;** Christchurch Place, Dublin 8; 01 677 8099; open hours vary, check website or call before visiting; closed 26 Dec; adm €10 (cathedral, crypt and treasury); www.christchurchcathedral.ie

Dublinia: **MAP C4;** Synod Hall, St Michael's Hill, Dublin 8; 01 679 4611; open 10:30am–5:30pm daily; last adm 1 hr before closing; adm €15, students and seniors €13.50, children €7.50, family €37 (combination tickets for Dublinia & cathedral available); www.dublinia.ie

■ Classical concerts are often held in the cathedral (check website for details).

🔟 ⭐ St Patrick's Cathedral

St Patrick's, the Protestant Church of Ireland's national cathedral and one of the most important pilgrimage sites, stands on an early Christian site where St Patrick is said to have baptized converts in a well in 450. Like Christ Church Cathedral, the original structure was made of wood. It was not until 1190, when Archbishop John Comyn founded St Patrick's, that it was rebuilt in stone and raised to the status of a cathedral.

1 Nave
St Patrick's is the longest medieval church in Ireland and the nave **(below)**, with its carved pillars, reflects these immense proportions.

2 North Transept
Hanging above the arches of the North Transept are a number of flags commemorating Irish men and women who died in the service of the British Army.

3 South Transept
This former chapter house features a beautiful stained-glass window and numerous monuments. Particularly interesting is that of Archbishop Marsh which has fine carvings by Grinling Gibbons.

4 Quire
The quire **(above)** is adorned with swords, banners and helmets. These represent the different knights of St Patrick who, until 1869, underwent their services of investiture in this chapel. Another memorial honours Duke Frederick Schomberg, slain during fighting at the Battle of the Boyne.

5 Minot Tower
Believed to have been built for defence purposes, the almost 50-m (147-ft), 14th-century Minot Tower **(below)** still looks out of kilter with the rest of the cathedral.

7 Boyle Monument

The vast monument for the eminent Boyle family **(left)** is overrun with painted figures of the children of Richard Boyle, first Earl of Cork.

8 Graves of Jonathan Swift and Stella

One of the first ports of call for many visitors to the cathedral are the graves of the satirist Jonathan Swift *(see p42)* and his beloved Stella, positioned in the nave beneath brass tablets.

9 The Door of Reconciliation

A row between two 15th-century earls, Kildare and Ormond, reached stalemate when Ormond barricaded himself in the chapter house. Kildare cut a hole in the door and offered to shake hands. From this incident came the expression "chancing your arm". The door, with its hole, is on display in the North Transept.

JONATHAN SWIFT

Jonathan Swift was born in Dublin in 1667 and was educated at Trinity College *(see pp12–13)*. In 1694, he took holy orders and moved to England as tutor to young Esther Johnson at Moor Park in Surrey. Esther was to become the beloved "Stella" of his writings. Despite a reputation as a wit and pamphleteer, his ecclesiastical career was his primary concern and, in 1713, Swift was appointed dean of St Patrick's. On his death in 1745, he bequeathed £12,000 to build Dublin's St Patrick's Hospital.

10 South Aisle

Memorials here honour renowned Irish Protestants of the 20th century. Douglas Hyde, Ireland's first president and founder of the Gaelic League, is aptly remembered in Irish.

NEED TO KNOW

MAP D5 ■ St Patrick's Close, Dublin 8 ■ 01 453 9472 ■ www.stpatricks cathedral.ie

Open 9:30am–5:30pm Mon–Fri, 9am–5:30pm Sat, 9–11am & 1–3pm Sun (Mar–Oct: until 6:30pm Sat; 4:30–6:30pm Sun)

Adm €8, students and seniors €7, family €18

■ Listen to the choir at the following services: matins Choral evensong (5:30pm Mon–Fri, 3:15pm Sun) and Eucharist (11:15am most Sun). Check the website for schedule.

6 Lady Chapel

At the east end of the church, this 13th-century building **(above)** was given over to the French Huguenots who arrived as refugees in the mid-17th century. They were allowed to worship here by the Dean and Chapter, and did so for almost 150 years.

TOP 10 ⭐ Guinness Storehouse

Ask the majority of people what they most associate with Ireland, and the likely answer will be Guinness. Together with whiskey, it is the national drink, famous for its malty flavour and smooth, creamy head. Arthur Guinness founded this immensely successful brewery in 1759; 250 years on, Guinness remains one the largest breweries in Europe and the beer is available in over 150 countries worldwide. The excellent exhibition at St James's Gate covers all aspects of the production, and ends with a free pint in the Gravity Bar.

② Brewing Process

It takes a full ten days to brew the perfect pint of Guinness. The roaster, kieve kettle and maturation vessel are brought to life using 3D-animated graphics.

③ History of Cooperage

Displays in this section **(above)** explain how expert coopers crafted the stout wooden barrels in times past. Metal casks have been used since the 1940s.

① Ingredients

The brewery tour begins with a dramatic introduction to each component of the black stuff: a massive barley pit, gleaming glass columns full of hops and yeast, and even a tumbling waterfall **(above)** to represent the most fundamental ingredient of all – water.

NEED TO KNOW

MAP A5 ■ St James's Gate, Dublin 8 ■ 01 408 4800 ■ www.guinness-storehouse.com

Open 10am–7pm Mon–Fri, 9:30am–8pm Sat (until 7pm Sun); Jul & Aug: 10am–8pm Mon–Fri; last adm 2 hours before closing

Adm €26, students €22, children €10 (under 4s free)

■ The Brewer's Dining Hall features an open kitchen and serves quiche, pies, signature beef and Guinness stew.

■ Hold on to the ticket– it enables you to claim your free pint.

■ The area around the Guinness Storehouse is isolated; take the "Do Dublin" Hop-on Hop-off bus to get there.

4 Arthur Guinness Story

An 18th-century doctor, footman and bartender recount the fascinating life and times of Arthur Guinness. He founded his brewery in 1759 owing to a bequest from his godfather – a Church of Ireland archbishop.

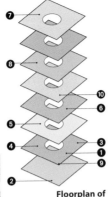

Floorplan of the Storehouse

Key to Floorplan
- Seventh floor
- Sixth floor
- Fifth floor
- Fourth floor
- Third floor
- Second floor
- First floor
- Ground floor

ARTHUR GUINNESS

In 1756, Arthur Guinness (1725–1803) first bought a lease on a brewery in Leixlip, near Dublin. Three years later, he gave this to his brother when he signed the lease for St James's Gate. He married Olivia Whitmore in 1761, and ten of their 21 children lived to establish a dynasty that has now expanded into many activities worldwide.

5 Tasting Rooms

This multi-sensory zone brings distinctive flavours to life. The bartenders demonstrate how to enjoy your drop – sip the black stuff, not the creamy head.

7 Gravity Bar

What most visitors wait for – the free pint at the Gravity Bar, with its 360° views.

8 Guinness and Food

There are three separate dining options here **(below)**, all with Guinness looming large on the menu.

9 Transport

This gallery **(above)** explores how Guinness has travelled the globe, and how it varies from nation to nation. It's now brewed in almost 50 countries – to the tune of 10 million glasses a day.

10 Guinness Academy

Learn how to pour the perfect pint here. The six-step ritual is as legendary as the beer itself – from the 119.5 seconds it takes to pour to the eventual settle.

6 Advertising

Immerse yourself in almost a century of ground-breaking campaigns, featuring film and TV ads, and an interactive iPad area.

TOP 10 ⭐ Kilmainham Gaol and Hospital

Despite sharing the same name, these two sights could not be more different, both in their appearance and history. The forbidding gaol was built in 1796, its damp and grim conditions adversely affecting the health of the inmates. The jail closed in 1924 and wasn't touched again until it was restored as a museum in the 1960s. Kilmainham Hospital, built in the 1680s, was modelled on Les Invalides in Paris. Now, it is home to the Irish Museum of Modern Art (IMMA).

1 Exhibition
Housed in a modern hall of the gaol, this exhibition **(above)** puts visitors in a rather gruesome mood for what follows. On the ground floor is a section on hanging techniques, while the bitter struggle for independence *(see p39)* is dealt with upstairs.

2 Gaol Chapel
The most poignant story related about the chapel here is the wedding of Joseph Plunkett and Grace Gifford. They married on the eve of Plunkett's execution, and were allowed 10 minutes alone together before Plunkett was taken out and executed.

3 West Wing
It doesn't take much to imagine the horror of internment here **(left)**. The guide tells of the conditions that the prisoners were subjected to – hard labour and only 1 hour of candlelight a night.

4 Tour
A tour covering Irish history from 1796 to 1924 covers the Stone Breaker's Yard, in which the leaders of the 1916 uprising *(see p39)* were executed by firing squad.

5 East Wing
A fine example of the "Panoptical" layout **(above)**, which is found in many Victorian prisons. The idea was to maximize light but allow for the constant surveillance of the prisoners.

6 Kilmainham Gate
This rather austere doorway is flanked by iron gates and sets the mood for a visit to the gaol. A tree-lined avenue links the fine surroundings of the Kilmainham Hospital to its much bleaker neighbour.

7 Gardens and Courtyard

Designed between 1710 and 1720, the hospital's splendid and beautifully kept formal gardens were laid out in the French style with herbs and medicinal plants. They were restored to their former glory in the 1980s.

8 Hospital Chapel

The magnificent Baroque ceiling with its cherub heads and vegetable swags, was unlike anything seen in Ireland at that time. James Tabary, a Huguenot settler, carved the altar, reredos and rails from Irish oak in 1686.

THE HISTORY OF KILMAINHAM HOSPITAL

Kilmainham's Royal Hospital was built between 1680 and 1684 to the designs of Sir William Robinson. It is considered the most important 17th-century building in Ireland. Built for retired veterans, the hospital was handed over to the Free State in 1922 and served as the Garda headquarters in 1930–1950. It was one of the first buildings to benefit from Dublin's restoration programme in the 1980s. Beautifully renovated, it reopened in 1991 as the IMMA.

10 Great Hall

Formerly the soldiers' dining room, the Great Hall is very grand. The portraits of monarchs and viceroys, commissioned between 1690 and 1734, are the earliest surviving collection of institutional portraits in Ireland.

NEED TO KNOW

MAP A6

Kilmainham Gaol: Inchicore Rd, Dublin 8; 01 453 5984; open: Apr, May & Sep: 9:30am–5:45pm daily (Jun–Aug: until 6pm; Oct–Mar: until 5:15pm); adm €8, seniors €6, children and students €4, family €20, free under 12s

IMMA: Royal Hospital, Military Rd, Dublin 8; 01 612 9900; open 10am–5:30pm Tue, Thu, Fri & Sat, 11:30am–5:30pm Wed, noon–5:30pm Sun and public hols; www.imma.ie

■ Some rooms of the hospital can be visited by guided tour only.

■ IMMA has a good café in the basement.

■ The hospital grounds are vast, with lovely views, and ideal for a picnic.

9 IMMA

Since its move here in 1991, the Irish Museum of Modern Art (IMMA) has made full use of the space available. There is a regularly changing resident collection of some 3,500 artworks (above), and contemporary art featuring in touring exhibitions.

TOP 10 ⭐ Phoenix Park

Surprisingly for such a small city, Phoenix Park is the largest enclosed city park in Europe. The name has no connection with the mythical bird but originates from the Gaelic *Fionn Uisce* which means "clear water" and refers to a spring that once existed here. Following the landscaping traditions of English parkland, complete with hundreds of deer, this is an idyllic place to escape from the bustling city centre. At the weekends, whole families spend the day here, indulging in a variety of activities from dog-walking to jogging, golf practice, hurling matches, cricket and polo.

1 Deerfield
This 18th-century house, in the centre of the park (below), was once the home of the British Chief Secretary for Ireland, Lord Cavendish, who was murdered in 1882 by an Irish nationalist. It is now the residence of the American ambassador.

2 Ashtown Castle
A visit to this tower house is included in the ticket to the Visitor Centre. It was once owned by the family of John Connell, who was an ancestor of Daniel O'Connell *(see p39)*. The tower was found inside the walls of the 18th-century Ashtown Lodge when the lodge was due to be demolished.

3 Magazine Fort
This fort became an arms depot after independence, but has been abandoned since the IRA raid in 1939, when more than one million rounds of ammunition were stolen.

4 Visitor Centre
The display here shows the changing face of the park, from 3500 BCE to the present day. It also features a reconstruction of the Knockmaree Cist grave, which was found in the park in 1838. On Saturday, free tours depart from here to Áras an Uachtaráin.

5 Áras an Uachtaráin
Designed by Nathaniel Clements, this fine Palladian house (above) from 1751 was the Vice-regal lodge. In 1938 it became the official home of the Irish president.

6 Phoenix Monument
Erected by the fourth Earl of Chesterfield in 1747, this column (left) is topped with what is meant to be a phoenix, but looks more like an eagle than the mythical bird.

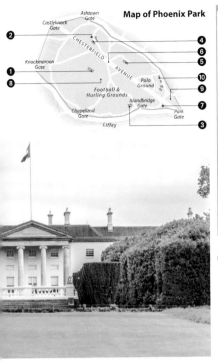

Map of Phoenix Park

⑨ People's Garden

Close to Park Gate, this is the only formal area of the whole park. Decimus Burton landscaped the area in the 1830s and the effect is gentle and restful, as the landscaped flowerbeds merge with the wilder hillocks and ponds.

⑦ Wellington Testimonial

Designed by Robert Smirke in 1817, the monument celebrates the victories of the Duke of Wellington, and is the tallest obelisk in Europe at over 62 m (200 ft).

⑧ Papal Cross

The simplicity of the 35-m (116-ft) high stainless steel Papal Cross is part of its beauty. It was erected on the spot where Pope John Paul II celebrated Mass in 1979.

⑩ Dublin Zoo

Dublin Zoo **(above)** dates back to 1831 – the fourth oldest in the world (see p46). The Kaziranga Forest Trail is modelled on a region in India. It is home to a growing herd of Indian elephants.

Top 10 of Everything

The elegant cocktail bar at Pichet

🔟 Moments in History

The Newgrange megalithic tomb, Ireland's prehistoric treasure

① Newgrange
The first settlers arrived in Ireland from the Continent around 7000 BCE, bringing with them farming skills and rudimentary tools. The megalithic stone tomb of the Stone Age at Newgrange *(see p76)* is believed to date from around 3200 BCE and is one of the most important passage graves in Europe.

② Celts Arrive
The Celts began to arrive in Ireland from Central Europe in around 500 BCE. With their ability to produce iron weapons and implements, the Celts soon imposed their culture and language.

③ Christianity Comes to Ireland
Although the Romans never settled in Ireland, it was through them that Christianity reached Irish shores. The first bishop was appointed in

St Patrick converting the Irish

431 but it was St Patrick *(see p44)* who is credited with the conversion of the pagan Celts and the establishment of the Church between 432 and 461.

④ Viking Ireland
The Vikings arrived in Ireland in 795 CE and established communities. In 1030, a wooden church *(see pp24–5)* was built where Christ Church Cathedral now stands.

⑤ First Irish Parliament
By the 1350s, the Normans had settled in Ireland and introduced the feudal system of government, led by a justiciar who was head of the army, chief judge and top administrator. He was helped in his work by a council of officials, and would occasionally summon a parliament consisting of his council, bishops, abbots and feudal lords. By the end of the 14th century, representatives of counties and towns were part of the process known as the Lower House, or Commons.

⑥ Battle of the Boyne
James II fled to France, after his defeat by William of Orange at the Battle of the Boyne in 1690, leaving Ireland in the hands of the Protestant Ascendancy. These were English descendants of Tudor and Stuart settlers. The native Irish suffered for more than a century from the penal measures inflicted on them.

7 Georgian High Culture

Many of the most important sights in the city, such as Custom House (see p40), were built in the Georgian era. Artists and musicians visited Dublin from all over Europe; one of the highlights was the premiere of Handel's oratorio, *The Messiah*, in Dublin in 1742.

8 The Great Famine

The potato famine dominated 19th-century Ireland. The crop failed first in 1845 as a result of potato blight. As a result, about two million people died of starvation or emigrated, many to America, in a period that lasted until 1852.

Irish emigrants bound for America

9 The Easter Rising

On Easter Monday 1916, Patrick Pearse and others, opposed to British rule, proclaimed the Declaration of Independence from the General Post Office (see p68). An uprising ensued. In December 1921 the Anglo-Irish treaty was signed, creating the Irish Free State.

10 The Referendums

In 2015, Ireland became the first country in the world to legalize same-sex marriage through a popular vote. The majority of the country (62 per cent) voted "yes" in a move that resulted in a giant street party in Dublin. Three years later, in 2018, Ireland voted "yes" once again, this time to legalize abortion, following a huge, country-wide campaign to Repeal the Eighth.

TOP 10 NOTABLE IRISH POLITICIANS

1 Henry Grattan
Grattan (1746–1820) entered Parliament in 1775 and was a great champion of the Catholic cause.

2 Theobald Wolfe Tone
Theobald Wolfe Tone (1763–98) was an Irish Republican and rebel who sought to overthrow English rule.

3 Daniel O'Connell
The greatest leader of Catholic Ireland, O'Connell (1775–1847) was a constant agitator against the Union.

4 Charles Stewart Parnell
Leader of the Irish Parliamentary Party in 1880, Parnell (1846–91) secured Gladstone's conversion to Home Rule.

5 Constance Markievicz
Markievicz (1868–1927) took part in the Easter Rising, and was the first woman elected into the UK House of Commons.

6 Patrick Pearse
Pearse (1879–1916) was executed for his involvement in the Easter Rising in 1916.

7 Michael Collins
Commander-in-Chief of the government forces in the Civil War, Michael Collins (1890–1922) was shot dead in his native County Cork.

8 Mary Robinson
Barrister Robinson (b.1944) was elected the first woman president of Ireland in 1990. She was in office until 1997.

9 Mary McAleese
Ireland's second female president, McAleese (b.1951) grew up in Northern Ireland during the Troubles, and helped to build bridges between the two countries.

10 Leo Varadkar
Varadkar (b.1979) was Ireland's youngest Taoiseach, and the first openly gay man to hold the position.

Former Taoiseach, Leo Varadkar

Historic Buildings and Monuments

City Hall's magnificent dome

1 City Hall

A competition was held in 1768 to select the designer of the Royal Exchange, and Thomas Cooley's plans were the preferred choice. One of Dublin's most sophisticated Georgian buildings (see p63), it marked the introduction to Ireland of the Neo-Classical architectural style, with its lofty dome supported by 12 columns and its 12 elegant circular windows.

2 Four Courts

MAP C3 ■ Inns Quay ■ 01 888 6459 ■ Open 10am–5pm (in session)

Designed by James Gandon in 1786, the magnificent Four Courts has a grand pedimented centre with arcaded screens and triumphal arches, topped with a colonnaded rotunda and a Neo-Classical dome. The five statues by Edward Smyth on the central block represent Moses, Wisdom, Authority, Justice and Mercy.

3 Dublin Castle

Originally rectangular in shape, Dublin Castle (see pp18–19) was designed as a "keepless castle", involving four circular corner towers and, midway along the south wall, a fifth tower. However, much of the medieval castle was destroyed by fire. The remodelling that you see today began at the turn of the 18th century.

4 Custom House

MAP G2 ■ Custom House Quay ■ 01 888 2000 ■ Open 10am–5:30pm daily

Designed by James Gandon and completed in 1791, the Custom House has four decorated façades, with finely balanced end pavilions and recessed Doric columns facing the River Liffey. Sculptor Edward Smyth created the fine statuary around the building. A fire destroyed much of the interior in 1921 during the War of Independence, but it was restored in the same decade. The latest restoration work was carried out in the 1980s.

Grand dome of the Four Courts building

Sir Edward Lovett Pearce designed the Palladian central block, with temple and portico flanked by colonnaded wings, in 1729; James Gandon contributed the portico to the east in 1785; and Robert Parke added the western portico. The Bank of Ireland took over the building in 1803.

8 Marsh's Library
MAP D6 ■ St Patrick's Close ■ Open 9:30am–5pm Tue–Fri; 10am–5pm Sat ■ Adm

Designed by Sir William Robinson of Kilmainham Hospital fame (see pp32–3) in 1701, this library was built to house the collection of Archbishop Narcissus Marsh. The Gothic-style battlements and entrance date from the 19th century, but the oak bookcases, arranged in bays between the windows, are original.

9 Famine Memorial
MAP G3

Cast in bronze by sculptor Rowan Gillespie, this memorial depicts figures staggering along Custom House Quay, from where many fled the Irish Potato Famine to North America in the 1840s. More than a million emigrated on ships such as the *Jeanie Johnston* (see p72), moored nearby.

Famine Memorial, Custom House Quay

5 The Spire
The world's tallest sculpture was erected on O'Connell Street in 2002. Its hollow stainless-steel cone rises 121 m (397 ft) above the cityscape, occupying the site once dominated by Nelson's Pillar (see p70), a monument to Admiral Horatio Nelson damaged by a terrorist bomb in 1966. At night its illuminated tip becomes a beacon. Dubliners have playfully lent it many nicknames, including the "Stiletto in the Ghetto".

6 Leinster House
MAP G5 ■ Kildare St ■ Visit by appt only

Designed by Richard Cassels for the Earl of Kildare in 1745, Leinster House is the home of the Irish parliament and is notable for its two contrasting façades, one resembling a townhouse, the other a country abode. The building was acquired by the State in 1924.

7 Bank of Ireland
MAP E4 ■ College Green

Built to accommodate the Irish House of Lords and House of Commons, the building is almost as magnificent as its English counterpart. Three architects were involved in its creation:

10 GPO Building
The work of Francis Johnston, the imposing General Post Office (see p68) opened in 1818. It holds a special place in Irish hearts as the spiritual birthplace of the Republic as rebels stormed the building on Easter Monday 1916, proclaiming independence.

🔟 Dublin Writers

1 Jonathan Swift

Swift (1667–1745) was born and educated in Dublin *(see p29)* and established a reputation as a wit through his satirical works. *A Modest Proposal* (1729), one of his most brilliant – if grim – satires, suggested feeding poor children to the rich. It is ironic that his work *Gulliver's Travels* (1726) is a children's classic.

2 Oscar Wilde

Wilde (1854–1900) was born at Westland Row, Dublin, and became a classics scholar at Trinity College *(see pp12–13)* and later at Oxford. His highly popular plays, include *An Ideal Husband* (1895) and *The Importance of Being Earnest* (1895). His imprisonment for homosexual offences inspired *The Ballad of Reading Gaol* (1898). He died, destitute in Paris, in 1900.

Sculpture of Wilde in Merrion Square

3 George Bernard Shaw

Born in Dublin, Shaw (1856–1950) moved to England in 1876. Initially a book reviewer for the *Pall Mall Gazette*, he went on to become a prolific playwright; *The Devil's Disciple* (1897) and *Pygmalion* (1913) are just two of his works. He received the Nobel Prize for Literature in 1925.

4 William Butler Yeats

W B Yeats (1865–1939), brother of the painter Jack B Yeats,

William Butler Yeats

was born in Dublin. His first volume of poetry, *The Wanderings of Oisin and Other Poems,* was well received and his later volumes confirmed his status as a leading poet. His play *On Baile's Strand* was chosen for the opening of Abbey Theatre *(see p70),* a much-lauded theatre, in 1904.

5 Sean O'Casey

Dublin-born Sean O'Casey (1880–1964) worked on the railways and became an active trade unionist. He achieved instant success with *The Shadow of a Gunman* (1923), which was set in the impoverished parts of Dublin, followed by the play *Juno and the Paycock* in 1924. His best-known work is from 1926, *The Plough and the Stars.*

6 James Joyce

The writer who most prolifically put Dublin on the literary map, Joyce (1882–1941) was born and educated in the city. He met Nora Barnacle on 16 June 1904 and, although they did not marry for 27 years, it became the date for events in his epic work *Ulysses*, published in Paris in 1922. *Dubliners* (1914), *Portrait of the Artist as a Young Man* (1916) and *Finnegans Wake* (1939) are among his other fine works.

Portrait of James Joyce, 1904

Irish novelist Elizabeth Bowen

7 Elizabeth Bowen

Although born in Dublin, Elizabeth Bowen (1899–1973) spent much of her childhood in Cork. Her years in wartime London are vividly evoked in her novels, including *The Heat of the Day* (1949).

8 Patrick Kavanagh

Kavanagh (1904–67), born in Monaghan, pursued a career as a journalist, poet and novelist first in London, and finally in Dublin. His reputation was established with a long and bitter poem on the hardships of rural life, *The Great Hunger* (1942).

9 Samuel Beckett

French Huguenot by descent, after a distinguished career at Trinity College, Beckett (1906–89) spent much of his life in France. The play *Waiting for Godot* (1952) made him an international name. He received the Nobel Prize for Literature in 1969.

10 Maeve Binchy

A treasured novelist in Ireland, Maeve Binchy (1939–2012) lived in the seaside village of Dalkey (*see p79*) for most of her life. An annual literary festival is held in her honour at Dalkey Castle (*see p78*).

TOP 10 IRISH WRITERS

1 William Trevor
William Trevor (1928–2016) was a master of the short story genre.

2 Brian Friel
The successes of playwright Friel (b. 1929) include *Dancing at Lughnasa* (1990).

3 Edna O'Brien
The Country Girls (1960) was the first novel by award-winning poet and novelist O'Brien (b.1930).

4 Frank McCourt
The evocative and tragicomic account of a tough, poverty-stricken upbringing in Limerick (*see p100*) in his memoir *Angela's Ashes* (1996) won McCourt (1930–2009) the Pulitzer Prize.

5 Seamus Heaney
Ireland's most prominent poet, Heaney (1939–2013) won the Nobel Prize for Literature in 1995. *North* (1975) explores the Troubles in Northern Ireland.

6 John Banville
A screenwriter, Banville (b.1945) is also a multi-award-winning novelist.

7 Colm Tóibín
Tóibín (b.1955) was shortlisted for the 2000 Man Booker Prize with his novel *The Blackwater Lightship* (1999).

8 Roddy Doyle
Renowned for his *Barrytown Trilogy* about Dublin life, Roddy Doyle (b.1958) also won the Man Booker Prize in 1993 for *Paddy Clarke Ha Ha Ha*.

9 Anne Enright
Anne Enright (b.1962) wrote the powerful novel *The Gathering* (2007), which won the prestigious Man Booker Prize.

10 Sally Rooney
A favourite of millennials, Sally Rooney (b.1991) has written three bestselling novels, all set mostly in Dublin.

Famous novelist, Sally Rooney

Irish Legends and Myths

(1) St Patrick

A 5th-century Roman Briton, St Patrick was captured by Irish raiders and taken into slavery in Ulster. Escaping back to Britain, he became a priest and returned to Ireland to help convert the Irish (*see p38*). Extraordinary tales about him abound – he cured the sick, raised the dead, and rid Ireland of snakes by ringing his bell.

St Patrick

(2) Punishment of the Children of Tuireann

The sun god Lugh demanded the three sons of Tuireann to give him magical objects and perform difficult feats as punishment for murdering his father. As their last task, they had to make three shouts from the Hill of Miochaoin.

(3) Cúchulainn

The boy Setanta had miraculous strength and loved the game of hurling. Invited to a feast by the legendary blacksmith Culain, Setanta arrived late and was met by the smith's ferocious guard dog. He killed the hound with his hurley stick and offered himself as a guard instead. He was renamed Cúchulainn, "hound of Culain".

(4) The Children of Lir

The greatest of the *Tuatha dé Danann*, or fairy folk, was the sea god Lir. His four beloved children were turned into swans by their jealous stepmother Aoife, who condemned them to live forever in the waters off the coast of Ulster. Around 900 years later, a Christian named Caomhog broke the spell, and baptized them as they died.

(5) Deirdre and the Exile of the Sons of Usnach

King Conchubar loved Deirdre, his harpist's beautiful daughter. The druid Cathbad foretold she would bring disaster, so her father kept her in solitude. But Deirdre loved Naoise, son of Usnach, who, with his brothers, took her to Scotland. After persuading them to return, Conchubar killed Usnach's sons. Deirdre, utterly grief-stricken, killed herself.

(6) Cattle Raid of Cooley

Connacht's Queen Medb (Maeve) raided Ulster to seize the chief Daire's famous bull. As all the men of Ulster were under a spell, Cúchulainn fought alone, killing all Medb's warriors and Medb had to retreat.

(7) Destruction of Dinn Ríg

Cobthach of Bregia killed his brother Lóegaire, the King of Leinster. Legends say that Moen, Lóegaire's grandson, was spared, but had to drink his grandfather's blood and was struck dumb. Later,

Children of Lir sculpture

Moen recovered his speech and was renamed Labraid ("speaks"). He eventually killed Cobthach by locking him in a house and burning him to death.

8 Oisin in Tír na nÓg

The son of Fionn mac Cumhaill, Oisin, and the daughter of sea god Manannan, Niamh, went to Tír na nÓg, the paradise of eternal youth. After 300 years, homesick Oisin borrowed Niamh's magic horse to visit Ireland. His feet were not to touch the ground, but he fell from the horse, instantly aged 300 years and died.

Oisin and Niamh in Tír na nÓg

9 Pursuit of Diarmuid and Grainne

Fionn mac Cumhaill asked King Cormac for his daughter, Grainne's hand in marriage, but she eloped with Fionn's nephew Diarmuid. The lovers were on the run for a year and a day with the enraged Fionn in pursuit.

10 Salmon of Knowledge

It was said that the first person to taste the Salmon of Knowledge would gain prophetic powers. Fionn mac Cumhaill visited Finnegas, the druid who caught the fish. Fionn's thumb touched the fish as it cooked, and as he put his thumb to his lips, he was the first to taste the fish.

TOP 10 CELTIC TRADITIONS

Celtic Crosses at Clonmacnoise

1 Celtic Crosses
High, richly carved stone crucifixes with a central circle are a feature of Celtic churches and monasteries.

2 Celtic Design
Distinctive traditional interlocking patterns and symbols that decorate ancient Celtic jewellery have always remained popular in Ireland.

3 Language
The Irish language, also known as Gaelic, is spoken by about 1.7 million people today, and comes directly from the ancient Celtic inhabitants.

4 Céilí
A large social get-together where people drink, sing, dance and stamp their feet to traditional Irish folk music.

5 Hurling
This robust Celtic game requires hurleys (ash sticks), a *sliotar* (a leather ball) and a large dose of energy.

6 Musical Instruments
Uillean pipes, *bodhráns* (drums), tin whistles and other Celtic instruments remain at the heart of Irish folk music.

7 St Brigid's Crosses
Country people still weave rushes into these crosses and hang them up to protect their home against evil spirits.

8 Fairy Trees
An isolated tree in a field is generally not cut down because it is often considered bad luck.

9 Water Worship
Sacred springs, fairy wells and holy water still play a large part in many Irish people's religious beliefs.

10 Craic
The witty, relaxed conviviality, gossip and talk that makes life worth living.

🔟 Children's Attractions

Wax models at Dublinia

1 Dublinia

Ancient Dublin is brought to life through vivid exhibits *(see p62)*. Fun interactive activities such as dressing up as a Viking, medieval games, and even discovering toothache remedies from 700 years ago, make up the Dublinia *(see p25)* experience.

2 Zipit

MAP N5 ▪ Tibradden Wood ▪ 051 858 008 ▪ Open Feb–Nov ▪ Adm ▪ www.zipit.ie

One of the three Zipit forest adventure centres in Ireland, this place offers exhilarating aerial assault courses with rope bridges, swinging logs and ziplines for ages seven and above. It is essential to book in advance.

3 Dublin Zoo

One of Ireland's top family attractions, Dublin Zoo *(see p35)* is a fun place to learn about wildlife. It's home to over 400 animals, all of whom have plenty of room to roam around. The zoo hosts a range of exciting, interactive and structured educational activities for children. It also supports conservation projects abroad and conducts some on site too, including breeding programmes.

4 National Aquatic Centre

Deanestown ▪ 01 646 4300 ▪ Open daily ▪ Adm ▪ www.nac.ie

In the northwestern suburbs, this mammoth facility, features many attractions. Parks and rides include the Aquazone water park with a wave pool, a surfing machine, lazy river, bubble pool, pirate ship play area (for eight years and under) along with massive water slides.

5 National Wax Museum Plus

MAP F3 ▪ 22–25 Westmoreland St ▪ 01 671 8373 ▪ Open 10am–7pm daily (last adm 6pm) ▪ Adm ▪ www.waxmuseumplus.ie

Kids will enjoy the "Wax World" featuring characters such as Harry Potter and Peppa Pig, while teens would love the Chambers of Horror. You can also take home a wax mould of your hand.

6 GPO Museum

Irish history is brought to life at the General Post Office *(see p68)*, which served as the headquarters for the leaders of the 1916 Rising. There are interactive games to play; you can have a go at writing newspaper reports or send a message using morse code.

⑦ National Leprechaun Museum

MAP D3 ▪ 1 Jervis St ▪ 01 873 3899 ▪ Open 10am–6:30pm daily (until 9pm Thu–Sat) ▪ Adm ▪ www.leprechaun museum.ie

Irish folklore is celebrated here with storytelling to give life to the local world of myth and legends. For ages 18 and above on Friday and Saturday evenings, they focus on folktales from the darker side of Ireland.

⑧ The Ark

MAP E4 ▪ 11a Eustace St ▪ Open daily ▪ Adm ▪ www.ark.ie

A purpose-built arts and cultural centre *(see p23)* where children can enjoy art and craft, pottery, theatre, workshops, concerts and more.

Children at the Ark

⑨ Airfield Estate

MAP T2 ▪ Dundrum ▪ 01 969 6666 ▪ Open hours vary, check website ▪ Adm ▪ www.airfield.ie

Dublin's only urban working farm, Airfield Estate has a range of daily activities, from egg collection to cow milking. The on-site restaurant is excellent, too.

⑩ Viking Splash Tour

MAP F5 ▪ Stephen's Green ▪ Open daily ▪ Adm ▪ www.viking splashdublin.ie

A military amphibious vehicle gives you a tour on land of the sights and scenes of Dublin before splashing into the Grand Canal Quay. The commentary is quirky and engaging.

Visitors aboard the Viking Splash boat

🔟 Performing Arts Venues

The plush, grand interior of The Olympia Theatre

1 The Olympia Theatre
MAP D4 ■ 72 Dame St ■ Box
office: 01 679 3323 ■ www.olympia.ie
Opened in 1879 as a music hall,
after years of rivalry with the Gaiety
Theatre, the Olympia settled down
to staging a very similar gamut of
musicals, live bands and comedy.

2 Abbey Theatre
The Abbey Theatre *(see p70)* is
a legend. Founded in the early 20th
century by a circle of writers such as
the poet W B Yeats, it gained renown
at the cutting edge of Irish theatre.
Controversial works by new writers
such as Sean O'Casey and J M Synge
were staged here, both causing riots
on opening night. Now classics, these
plays are the mainstay of the Abbey
stage, while experimental work is
shown on the Peacock stage.

3 Project Arts Centre
MAP D4 ■ 39 East Essex St
■ 01 881 9613 ■ www.projectarts
centre.ie
Built in the 60s as a spin-off project
to the Gate Theatre, the Project Arts
Centre is at the forefront of the artistic
life in Dublin, with a variety of young
companies exploring innovative
dance, music, drama and poetry.
U2, Liam Neeson and Gabriel
Byrne were all rising stars here.

4 The Gate Theatre
Since its founding in 1928,
the Gate *(see p72)* has been one of the
most daring theatres in Europe, intro-
ducing Irish audiences to Ibsen and
Chekhov, and Oscar Wilde's *Salome*
while it was banned in England. Orson
Welles, James Mason and Michael
Gambon began their careers here.

5 National Concert Hall
MAP F6 ■ Earlsfort Terrace
■ 01 417 0000 ■ www.nch.ie
Ireland's premier venue for quality
classical music, National Concert
Hall hosts guests of the calibre of the
New York Philharmonic. The building
is also home to Ireland's National
Symphony Orchestra. Jazz, contemporary and traditional Irish music are
also performed here, and there
are lunchtime concerts in summer.

The prestigious National Concert Hall

6 The Gaiety Theatre
MAP E5 ▪ S King St ▪ Box office: 081 871 9388 ▪ www.gaietytheatre.ie

Dublin's oldest theatre dating from 1871, this classical Victorian auditorium is an atmospheric backdrop for a wide range of entertainment, including musical theatre, opera and comedy.

7 Bewley's Café Theatre
MAP E5 ▪ Brewley's Café, 78/79 Grafton St ▪ 086 878 4001 ▪ www. bewleyscafetheatre.com

A unique opportunity for lunchtime drama from Monday to Saturday above Grafton Street's iconic café.

Smock Alley Theatre

8 Smock Alley Theatre
MAP D4 ▪ 6–7 Exchange St Lower ▪ 01 677 0014 ▪ www.smock alley.com

Founded in 1662, Smock Alley Theatre reopened in 2012 after a bold reconstruction. It has 17th-century walls in two performance spaces, and puts on a lively, mixed programme.

9 Bord Gais Energy Theatre
MAP D4 ▪ Grand Canal Sq ▪ 01 677 7999 ▪ www.bordgaisenergy theatre.ie

A striking, contemporary venue for West End touring productions, opera, ballet, theatre and popular music.

10 The Helix
MAP T2 ▪ Collins Ave, DCU, Glasnevin ▪ 01 700 7000 ▪ www. thehelix.ie

This venue hosts diverse theatre, opera and music productions.

TOP 10 CULTURAL EVENTS

1 Temple Bar TradFest
MAP E4 ▪ Temple Bar ▪ 01 960 2300 ▪ Late Jan ▪ www.tradfesttemple bar.com
Staged over five days, this is Dublin's biggest trad music and culture festival.

2 Dublin International Film Festival
Feb/Mar ▪ www.diff.ie
The DIFF celebrates the best of Irish and worldwide cinema.

3 St Patrick's Festival
A fun four-day series of events *(see p54)* surrounds the parade that takes place on the day.

4 Bloomsday
16 Jun
Fans of James Joyce re-enact his novel *Ulysses* on the day it is set.

5 Dublin International Chamber Music Festival
Jun
Chamber music events are held in grand venues around Ireland.

6 Galway International Arts Festival
MAP N3 ▪ Jul ▪ www.giaf.ie
Massive annual celebration of film, theatre, art, literature and music.

7 Dublin Fringe Festival
2 weeks in Sep
The Fringe includes dance, street performances, visual arts and comedy.

8 Dublin Theatre Festival
This two-week event *(see p54)* showcases Irish and international talent.

9 Wexford Opera Festival
MAP P5 ▪ Oct
Performances of different operas at Wexford's National Opera House.

10 Cork Jazz Festival
MAP Q3 ▪ End Oct
A popular festival with performances and events throughout the city.

Artists at the Cork Jazz Festival

TOP 10 Pubs

Kehoe's, with its old Victorian decor

1 Kehoe's

Just off Grafton Street, this pub *(see p66)* has lost none of its original character. It's usually busy, but there's a large snug to hide away in, just beside the entrance. Close to Trinity College, it attracts a mix of students and old pub characters. On Monday nights, there is live comedy upstairs at The Comedy Corner.

2 The Stag's Head

One of Dublin's literary pubs, The Stag's Head *(see p66)* was a regular haunt of James Joyce. This pleasant inn was refurbished in opulent Victorian style, with mirrors reaching up to the high ceiling, a counter topped with Connemara marble, plus, of course, the scary antlered namesake on the wall.

The venerable Stag's Head

3 Ryan's and F.X. Buckley

This beautifully preserved pub *(see p80)* with wonderful Victorian decor has self-contained snugs – originally for "the ladies" – on each side of the counter, and an oyster bar to accompany your Guinness. Upstairs is a cosy steak restaurant which has won several awards.

4 Doheny and Nesbitt

MAP G6 ■ 5 Lower Baggot St
■ Open hours vary, check website
■ www.dohenyandnesbitts.ie

Due to its location, this pub has been a hangout for politicos and journalists for more than a century. The Victorian ambience remains pleasingly intact.

Café en Seine's beautiful interior

5 Café en Seine

MAP F5 ■ 40 Dawson St
■ Open hours vary, check website
■ www.cafeenseine.ie

Decorated in French coffee-house style, the three floors of this large café-bar are filled with giant lamp-shades, mirrors, ornate sculptures and plants stretching up to the glass atrium. Expect queues on weekends.

6 Mulligan's

Once a working-class drinking man's pub (there were originally no chairs, since "real men" should stand as they drink), Mulligan's *(see p66)* has since attracted a mixed bag, including former US President John F Kennedy. It is still stark, but cosy nonetheless, and constantly busy.

The ancient Brazen Head pub

7 The Brazen Head
MAP C4 ▪ 20 Lower Bridge St
▪ Open hours vary, check website
▪ www.brazenhead.com

This pub, in the heart of Viking Dublin, is the oldest in the country, dating back to 1198. It has served a colourful set of patriots, including James Joyce, Brendan Behan, Van Morrison and Garth Brooks. The courtyard is a lovely spot for trying out one of the best pints of Guinness in Dublin and listening to live traditional Irish music.

8 The Long Hall
MAP E5 ▪ 51 S Great George's St
▪ Open daily

The Long Hall is mostly a locals' pub, although many visitors come to experience its evocative atmosphere. The decor includes chandeliers and a pendulum clock which is more than 200 years old.

9 O'Donoghue's
Music and fun are the lifeblood of this pub *(see p66)*, which fostered the popular balladiers, The Dubliners. Enjoy an informal music session, or, if the sun's shining, have a drink in the little courtyard out back.

10 The Porterhouse
Although it no longer brews its beer on site, this brewery pub *(see p66)* serves a great array of Porterhouse ales, such as the Renegade IPA or chocolate stout. There's live music on weekends.

TOP 10 NIGHTSPOTS

1 The International Bar
One of the best drinking spots in town, with regular live music nights and comedy shows *(see p66)*.

2 The Old Storehouse
MAP E4 ▪ 3 Crown Alley
Good beer and craic with two bands and live Irish music, nightly.

3 Copper Face Jack's
MAP E6 ▪ 29–30 Harcourt St
A lively and popular nightclub, Copper's is the place to let your hair down.

4 Krystle
MAP E6 ▪ 21–25 Harcourt St
Smart party venue with eclectic dance music to suit all tastes.

5 Vicar Street
MAP B4 ▪ 58–59 Thomas St
This trendy venue hosts live gigs, comedy shows, and traditional and rock music.

6 The Button Factory
MAP E4 ▪ Curved St, Temple Bar
One of the best live music venues in the city. Club nights Fri–Sat.

7 The Sugar Club
MAP F6 ▪ 8 Lower Leeson St
Great cocktails and everything from casino nights to jazz, hip-hop and salsa.

8 The Academy
MAP E3 ▪ 57 Middle Abbey St
Four thumping floors of music, from big-draw acts to smaller gigs.

9 The Workman's Club
MAP D3 ▪ 10 Wellington Quay
▪ 01 670 6692
A mishmash of live bands and DJs play between rooms in this cool spot.

10 Whelan's
MAP D6 ▪ 25 Wexford St
This exciting live venue is a favourite of many musicians, local and international.

Acoustic gig at Whelan's

🔟 Restaurants

1 Patrick Guilbaud

The first two-star Michelin restaurant in Ireland, Patrick Guilbaud *(see p67)* offers modern classic cuisine prepared with locally sourced ingredients. Guilbaud uses Ireland's bountiful fresh fish, meat and game to create savoury Gallic dishes. The restaurant is set in one of the townhouses that make up the sophisticated Merrion hotel *(see p128)*. Furnished in 18th-century style, it makes a great setting for this fine cuisine. Booking in advance is recommended.

The airy interior of Taste at Rustic

2 Taste at Rustic

The Japanese influence at celebrity chef Dylan McGrath's restaurant, Taste at Rustic *(see p67)*, goes way beyond sushi and sashimi. There are several separate menus to mix and match, which lean on the flavours of South American and Spanish cuisine to provide a veritable feast for the senses. The informal atmosphere is distinguished with its airy, high ceiling and exposed brick walls, along with accents of bare wood.

3 Mulberry Garden

It's well worth the short cab ride out to Donnybrook for this innovative little restaurant. Tucked away in a quaint century-old cottage and ripe with Irish flavour, everything at Mulberry Garden *(see p81)* – from the mineral water on the table to the

art on the walls – is locally sourced. The menu is fresh-from-market and changes weekly, with just three choices of starters, mains and desserts in traditional *table d'hôte* style, for €75 a head. The menu is accompanied by a well-thought out wine list and an excellent cheese board.

4 101 Talbot Street

A reputation for excellent, creative dishes at reasonable prices has helped 101 Talbot Street *(see p73)* to remain one of north Dublin's most popular restaurants. Menus feature classic Irish dishes such as fish pie and lamb rump.

5 Dax

It may not look all that special from the street, but in its Georgian basement Dax *(see p67)* gastronomically transports diners to a French country manor house. The interior is complete with hardwood ceilings and original flagstone floors. The food and wine are Gallic-influenced with added touches of homemade breads and ice creams. All in all, it's perfect for a romantic evening *à deux*.

The welcoming façade of the popular restaurant Pichet

6 Pichet

This vibrant, trendy and award-winning bistro *(see p67)* provides the perfect setting to enjoy delicious French-inspired dishes with an Irish twist, such as locally caught mussels in white wine and chargrilled monkfish with seaweed buttered potatoes. The cocktail bar also serves snacks. The wine list offers a good selection of craft beers and ciders, that are served in a glass or pichet.

7 Chapter One

The arched granite walls of this basement on Parnell Square are home to one of the city's finest restaurants, Chapter One *(see p73)*. Here they serve superb Irish cooking with classic French and Nordic influences, plus an unparalleled cheese trolley and an Irish coffee that is flambéed tableside.

8 PHX Bistro

A rare find, PHX Bistro *(see p73)* is a modern and cosy place where the friendly and efficient staff serve top-notch food. The menu offers dishes inspired from traditional Irish cuisine, with some European flavours thrown into the mix. The risottos and steaks are presented with a modern take, and the Irish farmhouse cheese slate rounds off the meal perfectly.

9 Trocadero

Held in high esteem by locals and visitors alike, Trocadero *(see p67)* is the archetypal Dublin theatre restaurant. The decor offers much to talk about with famous stage personalities, who have dined here, gazing down from its dark walls. Try the excellent steak and stay late to soak up the welcoming atmosphere. "The Troc" really comes alive when the post-theatre crowd arrives.

Gnocchi topped with truffle, Etto

10 Etto

Five minutes' walk from St Stephen's Green, Etto *(see p67)* is a small, cool bistro that's a favourite among many of Dublin's top chefs. The menu here changes each day. Expect to see French-Irish dishes such as *côte de boeuf* (beef rib steak) and a dessert of red wine prunes with mascarpone. Advance booking is recommended.

🔟 Festivals and Events

Ireland in the Six Nations Rugby

1 Six Nations Rugby
MAP T2 ■ Lansdowne Rd ■ Feb–Mar ■ www.sixnations rugby.com

The Aviva Stadium is the Irish venue for this annual competition between Ireland, England, France, Italy, Wales and Scotland. Initially formed as the Home Nations Championship in 1883, Six Nations Rugby has happened every year, except during the World War II.

2 St Patrick's Festival
MAP M5 ■ Mar 17 ■ www.st patricksfestival.ie

Usually spanning four days around Ireland's national holiday, the St Patrick's celebrations (see p49) are every bit as riotous as you'd expect. There's a giant parade, fireworks and a daily rota of gigs at the Festival Stage in Collins Barracks.

3 Colours Boat Race
MAP F3 ■ Mar/Apr ■ www. coloursboatraces.ie

Crowds flock to the Liffey as Trinity and University College Dublin compete in the age-old rivalry of a rowing race between O'Connell Bridge and St James's Gate.

4 Women's Mini Marathon
MAP G6 ■ Early Jun ■ www. vhiwomensminimarathon.ie

Attracting around 40,000 participants, this 10-km- (6-mile) all-female sporting event raises thousands for charity through sponsored runners.

5 Dublin Pride
MAP E2 ■ Jun ■ www.dublin pride.ie

With music concerts, club nights and an epic parade, Dublin Pride is celebrated with gusto all around the city. The festival is usually around ten days long.

6 All-Ireland Hurling Final
MAP T2 ■ Croke Park ■ Aug ■ www.crokepark.ie

The world's oldest field sport, hurling requires a huge amount of skill to control a speeding ball with a hurley. As it is also the Irish national sport, the Hurling Final is a popular event.

7 Big Grill Festival
MAP N5 ■ Herbert Park ■ Aug ■ www.biggrillfestival.com

The wonderful Big Grill brings the world's top BBQ chefs to Dublin, and hosts a mix of food stalls, demonstrations and masterclasses.

8 Dublin Theatre Festival
MAP D4 ■ Late Sep–Oct ■ www.dublintheatrefestival.ie

With a focus on Dublin-centric plays and writers, this theatre festival (see p49) attracts the world's finest to the capital for two weeks of productions. The Dublin Fringe Festival also runs in September.

Parade at the New Year's Eve Festival

9 Dublin Marathon
MAP G6 ■ Last Sun in Oct
■ www.kbcdublinmarathon.ie

Winding through the historic streets of the city, the Dublin Marathon attracts thousands of spectators. It starts at Fitzwilliam Street Upper and winds down to conclude at Merrion Square, covering 41 km (26 miles) of the city, looping past University College Dublin and Bushy Park to Pheonix Park.

Participants in the Dublin Marathon

10 New Year's Eve Festival
MAP H3 ■ North Wall Quay ■ 31 Dec
■ www.nyfdublin.com

The New Year is rung in with a series of music concerts in the Festival Village, on the edge of the River Liffey. At midnight, a massive firework display marks the moment, before the party continues elsewhere.

TOP 10 MOMENTS IN IRISH SPORT

McGuigan challenges Pedroza

1 1978
Munster rugby team defeats the All Blacks.

2 1985
Barry McGuigan wins world featherweight boxing title.

3 1987
Stephen Roche wins the Tour de France, Giro d'Italia and World Championship in a single season.

4 1990
Penalty shootout win over Romania in the Italia 90 World Cup.

5 2000
Sonia O'Sullivan clinches silver in 5000 metres at the Olympics in Sydney.

6 2011
Rory McIlroy wins the US Open, with a record 16 strokes under par.

7 2012
Lightweight boxer Katie Taylor from Bray wins gold at the 2012 Olympics in London.

8 2013
Tony McCoy clocks up an unprecedented 4,000th win on Mountain Tunes in the Weatherbys Novices' Hurdle race at Towcester.

9 2016
Brothers Gary and Paul O'Donovan won Ireland's first ever Olympic medal in rowing, with silver at the Rio de Janeiro Games.

10 2018
Ireland clinches an historic win over New Zealand and wins the Rugby Grand Slam in the Six Nations Championship. Ireland also makes the Ladies' Hockey World Cup final despite being ranked the second worst team.

TOP10 Dublin for Free

National Gallery of Ireland

1 Art for Free
Both the classic canvases at the National Gallery *(see pp16–17)* and the cutting-edge contemporary works at IMMA *(see p33)* are free to view. Tour the eye-catching street art in Smithfield and Temple Bar, where James Earley's massive *Ulysses* mural adorns the façade of Blooms Hotel.

2 Free Fiddling
No trip to Dublin is complete without some traditional Irish music, whether it's a spirited gig at O'Donoghue's *(see p51)* or one of the long-running open trad sessions in the Cobblestone *(77 King St N)*, a self-proclaimed "drinking pub with a music problem".

3 A Walk Through Trinity
Strolling the cobbled quads of Trinity College can fill a morning or afternoon, especially if you stop at the excellent Douglas Hyde Gallery *(see p12)* for free art exhibitions.

4 The Famine Memorial
Dublin's most moving monument *(see p41)* is a little off the tourist track, on Custom House Quay. This unflinching family of sculptures by Rowan Gillespie remembers the victims of the 1840s famine, which killed a million Irish people and led two million more to emigrate, many on ships to America from the nearby docks.

5 Park Life
Dublin abounds with green spaces, and vast Phoenix Park *(see pp34–5)*, originally established as a royal deer park in the 17th century, tops the bill with its free Visitor Centre housing a historical interpretation of the park through the ages, and Victorian teahouse. Farmleigh Estate, in the park's northwest corner, features attractive ornamental gardens, free house tours and frequent food and craft markets.

6 Free Laughs
MAP E4 ■ 1 Dame Court ■ 01 679 3687 ■ www.stagshead.ie
Laughs are guaranteed at the Stag's Head *(see p66)* pub every Sunday and Monday night. Not only are its popular "Comedy Crunch" stand-up shows free, you get a complementary ice cream thrown in, too.

7 Guided Tour
www.dublinfreewalkingtour.ie
"Drink, music, literature and sex" are all on the menu on a 3-hour outing with the Dublin Free Walking Tour. Its daily trips take in the popular tourist spots south of the river; the 3:30pm

The Campanile, Trinity College

walk heads north, off the beaten track. Both start from the Spire *(see p41)* on O'Connell Street.

(8) A Day at the Seaside

With its gardens, pier and breeze-blown headland hikes, Howth *(see p78)* is Dublin's best day by the sea. Get there on the Dart from the city centre, and dally on the harbour to watch seals sport when the fishing boats come in. Top it off with fish and chips at Beshoff Bros *(12 Harbour Rd)*.

Yachts docked in Howth harbour

(9) People-Powered

Temple Bar's nerve centre for people-watching is Meeting House Square *(see p22)*, whose vibrant Saturday food market under the umbrellas is a winner. There's a free outdoor cinema season there every summer: bag tickets from the office opposite the Photographic Archive.

(10) See the Skulls

MAP T2 ■ Finglas Rd, Glasnevin ■ www.glasnevintrust.ie

Dublin's churches are packed with fascinating memorials: romantics should try the Whitefriar Street Carmelite Church, with its relics of St Valentine. Most rewarding of all is Glasnevin Cemetery *(see p76)*, lined with tombs of Ireland's great and good. The nearby National Botanic Gardens are free, too.

TOP 10 BUDGET TIPS

1 All Dublin's national museums, galleries and libraries are free, while most paid attractions offer about a third off ticket prices for children, students and over-60s.

2 The Dublin Pass (1, 2, 3, 4 or 5 days) covers entry to over 30 attractions, a skip-the-queue facility and a 24-hour Hop-on Hop-off bus tour (www.dublinpass.com).

3 A special, pre-paid Leap Visitor Card offers unlimited travel on all bus, tram and Dart trains in and around Dublin (www.leapcard.ie).

4 Trekker and Explorer tickets offer unlimited train travel for 4 consecutive days and any 5 days in 15, respectively (www.irishrail.ie/fares-and-tickets).

5 Intercity bus travel is cheaper still: book online for discounted rates and a guaranteed seat *(www.buseireann.ie)*.

6 Travel off-season to save money: prices get hiked on rugby inter-national weekends *(see p54)*, St Patrick's Festival *(see p49)* and bank holidays.

7 Look out for early-bird specials at city restaurants: many offer discounted menus if you eat before 7pm.

8 Trinity College lets 600 rooms in summer from €85 per night (www.tcd.ie).

9 Download the free Dublin Discovery Trails app, offering five self-guided routes (www.visitdublin.com).

10 Dublin Bikes offers on-street rental scheme, and rides of up to 30 minutes are free. Register with a credit card at one of 115-plus bike pick-up points across the city (www.dublinbikes.ie).

Bicycles for rent in Dublin

Dublin and Ireland Area by Area

Ha'penny Bridge, spanning the banks of the River Liffey, Dublin

🔟 South of the Liffey

Dublin takes its name from the southwest of the city when, in prehistoric times, there was a dark pool *(Dubh Linn)* at the confluence of the River Liffey and what was once the River Poddle. The area expanded during the 18th century, when the cobbled streets of Temple Bar became a centre for merchants and craftsmen – interestingly, reverting to similar use in the 20th century. Prior to the founding of Trinity College in 1592, southeast Dublin was undeveloped. St Stephen's Green wasn't enclosed until the 1660s and it remained for private use until 1877. But from the 1850s the area witnessed a building boom. Today, the south is the hub of the fashionable scene, with designer stores and fine restaurants.

A page from the *Book of Kells,* **Trinity College**

SOUTH OF THE LIFFEY

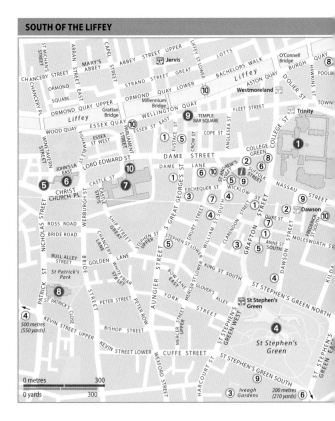

1 Trinity College

Ireland's premier institute of education was founded in 1592 by Queen Elizabeth I on the site of an Augustinian monastery. At its start, a Protestant-only college, Trinity *(see pp12–13)* opened its doors to Catholic students in 1793, but it wasn't until the 1970s that the Catholic Church relaxed its opposition to the college. Its quadrangles are peaceful havens, and its priceless *Book of Kells* a highlight.

2 National Gallery of Ireland

This gallery *(see pp16–17)* houses the National Art Collection and stages temporary exhibitions as well as artist-led workshops. The gallery also provides family tours for interested children. Other facilities include a large shop, a café and restaurant, and several lecture theatres.

3 National Museum of Ireland

Only two of the museum's *(see pp14–15)* three sites are south of the river: the Natural History Museum *(see p64)* and the branch on Kildare Street *(see p14)* which examines Irish archaeology and antiquities. The latter's 19th-century building, with marble and mosaics, is almost as impressive as the collections.

National Museum of Ireland

4 St Stephen's Green
MAP F6

At the foot of Grafton Street, St Stephen's Green is Dublin's primary pleasure ground with nine hectares of landscaped Victorian lakes and gardens, plus winding footpaths, a children's playground and bandstand. There are monuments to Joyce, Yeats and Wolf Tone, and a tour of the park leaves the nearby Little Museum of Dublin at 11:30am on Saturdays and Sundays. The museum *(open 10am–5pm daily; adm)* is well worth a look, too – a lively sprint through the city's 20th-century history, stuffed with more than 5,000 artifacts donated by real-life Dubliners. Rock fans will enjoy the room dedicated to Irish megastars U2, on the top floor.

CITY OF CULTURE

Dublin's southside is the embodiment of the city's regeneration as a cultural hub for the 21st century. Numerous names associated with style and glamour have contributed to this trend. The Irish rock band U2 own the stylish Clarence hotel *(see p128)*. Designers Philip Treacy and Orla Kiely as well as pop icons Bono and Enya have made the city their home.

5 Dublinia

Set in the Neo-Gothic Synod Hall, part of Christ Church Cathedral *(see pp24–5)*, Dublinia *(see p25)* brings the ancient city to life through inter-active galleries, complete with sounds, smells and costumed interpreters. Experience life aboard a Viking war-ship before moving on to the medieval zone, with its merchant's kitchen and bustling fair. Major events in Dublin's history, such as the Black Death and the rebellion of Silken Thomas, are also portrayed here *(see p46)*. The visit ends atop St Michael's Tower, with views across Dublin.

6 Christ Church Cathedral

One of the city's two great cathedrals *(see pp24–5)*, illustrating the impor-tance religion has always played in Dublin life, Christ Church was the first to be built, in 1030. Although nothing of the original wooden church stands now, there are plenty of beautiful medieval floor tiles and stone carvings. The treasures of Christ Church exhibition, in the 12th-century crypt, include a gilt plate donated by William of Orange in 1697.

7 Dublin Castle

Built into the city walls in 1204, the castle *(see pp18–21)* was Dublin's greatest stronghold, designed to defend the British-ruled city against the native Irish. It was at that time protected by rivers on both sides, the Liffey to the north and the Poddle to the south. The castle was completely rebuilt after a fire in 1684 and was further refined during the Georgian period, from which time most of the state apartments date.

The nave of St Patrick's Cathedral

8 St Patrick's Cathedral

Dublin's "second" cathedral and long-time rival to Christ Church, St Patrick's *(see pp28–9)* is decorated with busts, brasses, monuments and plaques commemorating deceased dignitaries, and architectural features. Many visitors come to see the associ-ation with Jonathan Swift *(see p29)*. Memorabilia include his death mask, writing desk and chair, and the memorial to himself and Stella.

Panoramic view of the Christ Church Cathedral

Temple Bar with its lively pubs

⑨ Temple Bar

This hugely popular area (see pp22–3), on the banks of the Liffey (the term "bar" means a riverside path), is the heart of south Dublin and has a seemingly limitless array of pubs, restaurants and bars as well as interesting little shops, galleries and cultural centres, such as Photo Museum Ireland and the Irish Film Institute. Its bustling, vibrant atmosphere, lively nightlife, trendy businesses and hip residents and clientele are the personification of Dublin's emergence as one of Europe's most fashionable and popular cities.

⑩ City Hall

MAP D4 ■ Cork Hill, Dame St
■ Open 10am–4pm Mon–Sat

Thomas Cooley designed this stately building, with its distinctive copper dome, between 1769 and 1779. He had won the commission as a result of a competition, beating his better-known contemporary James Gandon, who designed the Four Courts and Custom House (see p40). It was originally built as the city's Royal Exchange. City bureaucrats latterly used it for various purposes but, having undergone extensive restoration in the early 2000s, it is now open to the public. There is an excellent permanent exhibition in the reconstructed vaults entitled "The Story of the Capital", covering 1,000 years of Dublin's history.

▶ **MORNING**

Have breakfast in style at **The Westbury** (see p128) then go on to spend the first half of the morning exploring the many shops on Grafton Street and in Powerscourt Townhouse (MAP E4; 59 South William St), and soaking up the atmosphere of the street entertainers. Once the crowds move in, continue down to College Green and walk under the arch into **Trinity College** (see pp12–13) to relax in the grounds. On leaving Trinity, head down Dame Street to **Temple Bar** (see pp22–3) and enjoy the many shops and galleries here.

For lunch, press on to **Leo Burdock's** (2 Werburgh St), the city's oldest fish-and-chip shop. It serves take-away only so make for **Christ Church Cathedral** (see pp24–5) and sit and admire its exterior while eating. Then wander inside to view the restored crypt and treasury.

AFTERNOON

After lunch, retrace your steps to **Dublin Castle** (see pp18–21) for a tour of state apartments and a visit to the **Chester Beatty** (see pp18–21). A cup of eastern-flavoured coffee and a slice of baklava in the Silk Road Café here will set you up for the final stretch: walk west (or hop on the 123 bus) for a tour and a pint at the **Guinness Storehouse** (see pp30–31). Finally, make for the **Brazen Head** (see p51), on Lower Bridge Street, Dublin's oldest pub, or check out an evening concert at **St Patrick's Cathedral** (see pp28–9).

See map on pp60–61

The Best of the Rest

1 Photo Museum Ireland

Established in 1978 by John Osman as a not-for-profit organization, the changing exhibitions at Photo Museum Ireland *(see p23)* showcase the best of contemporary Irish and International photography.

2 Government Buildings
MAP G5 ■ Upper Merrion St
■ Open Sat (tours only)

Before independence, these buildings served as the Royal College of Science.

Water feature in the Iveagh Gardens

3 Iveagh Gardens
MAP E6

These little-known gardens are a lovely place to relax beside the roses.

4 Teeling Whiskey Distillery
MAP C6 ■ 13–17 Newmarket
■ Open noon–7pm daily ■ Adm

The jaunty tours of this traditional distillery include a tutored tasting.

5 Irish Rock 'n' Roll Museum Experience
MAP E4 ■ Curved St ■ Open 10:30am–5pm daily ■ Adm

Strum a guitar and see memorabilia from U2, Thin Lizzy and more.

6 Natural History Museum
MAP G5 ■ Merrion St
■ Open 10am–5pm Tue–Sat, 1–5pm Sun & Mon

A remarkable collection of taxidermied animals and skeletons illustrate the natural world through the ages at this branch *(see pp14–15)*.

7 National Library
MAP F5 ■ Kildare St
■ Closed Sun am

With its free exhibitions, lectures, performances and a cosy café, there's much more to the National Library than just books.

8 Merrion Square
MAP G5

One of the grandest of the city's Georgian squares, Merrion Square is lined with stately buildings. Oscar Wilde is one of the many illustrious past residents of the square.

9 Museum of Literature Ireland
MAP F6 ■ 86 St Stephen's Green
■ Open 10:30am–6pm Tue–Sun ■ Adm

Exploring Ireland's literary heritage, the Museum of Literature Ireland (MoLI) covers the works of various Irish writers. Visitors can also see the beautiful walled gardens at the back.

10 Ha'penny Bridge
MAP E3

The Ha'penny Bridge was built in 1816 to link the north and south sides of the Liffey, and a halfpenny toll was once charged to cross it.

Ha'penny Bridge over the Liffey

Southside Shops

1 Brown Thomas

MAP E4 ■ Grafton St

The smartest department store in town. A couple of floors of designer labels give the fashionistas plenty of scope, and there's also a wonderful glass and china department featuring top Irish designs.

2 Hodges Figgis
MAP F4 ■ 56–8 Dawson St

Established in 1768, this is Ireland's oldest bookshop mentioned in the famous *Ulysses*. The floors are full of books covering all subjects and very good bargains are available.

3 Kilkenny Shop
MAP F4 ■ 6 Nassau St

The best of Irish contemporary design in fashion, art, ceramics and glass is available here at reasonable prices, so it is a great place to pick up a unique souvenir.

Exterior of the Celtic Whiskey Shop

4 Celtic Whiskey Shop
MAP F5 ■ 27–8 Dawson St

Choose from a vast array of local Irish whiskeys as well as more famous brands. The service is as warm as a nip of the *uisce beatha* ("water of life").

5 Charles Byrne Musik Instrumente

MAP E5 ■ 21–22 Lower Stephen's St

From traditional instruments to novelty items like mini chocolate pianos, this family-owned shop dating to 1870 has plenty of gift ideas.

Freshly baked desserts at Avoca

6 Avoca

MAP E4 ■ 11–13 Suffolk St

An Aladdin's cave with beautiful and contemporary homeware – blankets, throws and cushions – alongside gorgeous own-label fashions. There's also an excellent food section, with a restaurant on the top floor and a deli in the basement.

7 Irish Design Shop
MAP E4 ■ 41 Drury St

This tiny shop is dedicated to all things design. A wide range of goods are offered here, from handwoven mohair scarves to quirky ceramics. It also sells gold jewellery that is made on site.

8 James Fox
MAP F4 ■ 119 Grafton St

A Dublin institution, James Fox's cigarette and cigar emporium is definitely a place for connoisseurs. It specializes in Cuban and other fine cigars, plus there's an extensive range of smoking accessories.

9 Kevin & Howlin
MAP F4 ■ 31 Nassau St

A traditional shop, with wonderful old-fashioned service, selling handwoven Irish tweeds and accessories for men and women, including the famous Donegal tweed.

10 DesignYard Gallery
MAP F5 ■ 25 South Frederick St

An excellent gallery shop with highly original pieces of contemporary Irish and European jewellery, sculpture and art by over 100 designers. Visits are by appointment only.

See map on pp60–61

Pubs and Bars

① Kehoe's
MAP F5 ■ 9 S Anne St
■ www.kehoesdublin.ie

One of the city's most popular pubs, Kehoe's (see p50) has an old-style wooden interior with a long bar, snug and stained-glass doors. Step in for the everflowing craic and one of the best pints in Dublin.

O'Neills, a traditional old Irish pub

② O'Neills
MAP E4 ■ 2 Suffolk St
■ www.oneillspubdublin.com

With an Old Irish exterior and a cosy and atmospheric interior, this pub is divided into several different areas. A great selection of whiskeys and craft beers is available alongside delicious oysters.

③ McDaids
MAP E5 ■ 3 Harry St ■ 01 679 4395

This pub offers literary tradition and a classic Dublin drinking experience. The writer Brendan Behan used to drink here, and it's a stop-off for a popular literary pub crawl.

④ Grogan's Castle Lounge
MAP E4 ■ 15 South William St
■ www.groganspub.ie

This friendly drinkers' joint is lined with local art, propped up by local characters, and locally feted for serving the best drop of Guinness in town. Decent toasties, too.

⑤ The International Bar
MAP E4 ■ 23 Wicklow St
■ 01 677 9250

Popular with writers and musicians. The evenings of live music and comedy here (see p51) are exceptionally good and well-attended.

⑥ The Stag's Head
MAP E4 ■ 1 Dame Court, off Dame St ■ www.stagshead.ie

Enjoy Irish food and music at The Stag's Head (see p50), which offers delicious bar snacks accompanied with beers.

⑦ Davy Byrne's
MAP F5 ■ 21 Duke St
■ www.davybyrnes.com

A friendly pub immortalized by James Joyce in his book *Ulysses*. Seafood and Irish fare accompany the drinks here.

⑧ Mulligan's
MAP F3 ■ 8 Poolbeg St
■ www.mulligans.ie

Established in 1782, Mulligan's (see p50) is one of Dublin's most popular watering holes.

⑨ O'Donoghue's
MAP F6 ■ 15 Merrion Row
■ www.odonoghues.ie

Witness traditional live Irish music here every night of the week (see p51).

⑩ The Porterhouse
MAP D4 ■ 16 Parliament St
■ www.theporterhouse.ie

A must visit for beer connoisseurs, The Porterhouse (see p51) opened in 1996 as the city's first micro-brewery.

Places to Eat

PRICE CATEGORIES
For a three-course meal for one with half a bottle of wine (or equivalent meal), taxes and extra charges.

€ under €45   €€ €45–€90   €€€ over €90

1 Pitt Bros
MAP E4 ■ 84–88 Great Georges St ■ 01 677 8777 ■ www.pittbrosbbq.com ■ €

A must for meat lovers, Pitt Bros is known for generous portions. Its signature style is slow-cooked smoked meat, with brisket and pulled pork.

2 Patrick Guilbaud
MAP G6 ■ 21 Merrion St Upper ■ 01 676 4192 ■ Open Tue–Sat ■ €€€

Patrick Guilbaud

One of Ireland's top restaurants, Patrick Guilbaud (see p52) serves French haute cuisine with a modern Irish twist. Try the set lunch menu.

3 Taste at Rustic
MAP E4 ■ 17 South Great George's St ■ 01 526 7701 ■ Closed Mon, Tue & Sun ■ €€

This modish restaurant (see p52) offers sensational combinations of flavours in their extensive menu. There is a tasting menu too.

4 The Port House
MAP E4 ■ 64 South William St ■ 01 677 0298 ■ www.porthouse.ie ■ €

A little corner of Spanish heaven in the heart of Dublin – this cosy candlelit restaurant serves a wide selection of tapas to the pulse of Spanish music. Tasty, affordable fare and good, friendly service.

5 Bunsen
MAP F5 ■ 3 Anne St South ■ 01 652 1022 ■ www.bunsen.ie ■ €€

Enjoy juicy, flavour-packed burgers, served in a casual, unpretentious setting at this restaurant.

6 Dax
MAP T2 ■ 23 Pembroke St Upper ■ 01 676 1494 ■ Closed Sun–Tue ■ www.dax.ie ■ €€

Set in the heart of Dublin's Georgian quarter, Dax (see p52) serves Franco-Irish cuisine in a country-style setting.

7 The Vintage Kitchen
MAP F3 ■ 7 Poolbeg St ■ 01 679 8705 ■ Closed Mon & Sun ■ €€

This relaxed dining room does exemplary locally sourced dishes. Bring your own wine, and corkage is just €5.

8 Etto
MAP G6 ■ 18 Merrion Row ■ 01 678 8872 ■ Closed Mon & Sun ■ €€

An ethos of simple ingredients cooked well has earned this restaurant (see p53) a legion of fans.

9 Trocadero
MAP E4 ■ 4 St Andrew's St ■ 01 677 5545 ■ www.trocadero.ie ■ €€

A great dining stalwart (see p53) with traditional fare. Try the excellent steak.

10 Pichet
MAP E4 ■ 14–15 Trinity St ■ 01 677 1060 ■ Closed Mon–Sat L ■ www.pichet.ie ■ €€

This bright, trendy bistro (see p53) serves modern cocktails and snacks at the bar, as well as Mediterranean and French dishes at the restaurant.

Chic interior of Pichet

See map on pp60–61

🔟 North of the Liffey

When Dublin was developed in the 18th century, plans for the north side of the River Liffey included a range of elegant terraces and squares designed to attract the city's elite. A downturn in the economy left the plan incomplete, although O'Connell Street and Parnell and Mountjoy squares remain evidence of what might have been. The area has some of the city's most beautiful buildings, such as the Custom House and the Four Courts; two theatres, the Abbey and Gate, which produce drama of worldwide acclaim; and the James Joyce Cultural Centre, which celebrates the life of the city's greatest writer.

The Neo-Classical General Post Office

1 General Post Office
MAP E2 ■ O'Connell St
■ Open 10am–5pm Tue–Sat ■ Adm
■ www.gpowitnesshistory.ie

Designed in 1814 by Francis Johnston, the GPO (see p46) is one of the city's most imposing buildings. It was the centre of the Easter Rising in 1916 and the scars of gunfire can still be seen on the Ionic portico. The history is traced in a sequence of paintings in the foyer by Irish artist Norman Teeling and also in the multimedia GPO Witness History experience.

NORTH OF THE LIFFEY

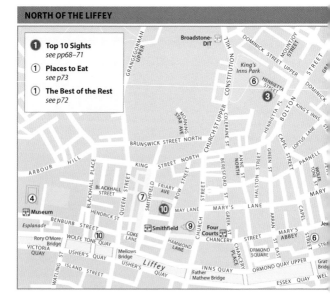

1 **Top 10 Sights**
see pp68–71

1 **Places to Eat**
see p73

1 **The Best of the Rest**
see p72

Tranquil setting of Parnell Square

③ 14 Henrietta Street
**MAP D1 ■ 14 Henrietta St
■ 01 524 0383 ■ Open 10am–
4pm Wed–Sun ■ Adm ■ www.14
henriettastreet.ie**

This museum, located, as the name suggests, on Henrietta Street, brings to life one of Dublin's Georgian buildings and its journey from a grand townhouse to a tenement. It connects the stories of the people who lived at this address over a 300-year period, with guided tours providing fascinating insights.

② Parnell Square
MAP E1

The credit for this lovely Georgian square goes to Bartholomew Mosse, who founded the Rotunda Hospital here *(see p72)*. It was considered one of Dublin's smartest addresses in the 1760s, then its fortunes declined, but it remains home to some fine restaurants and art galleries.

④ James Joyce Cultural Centre
**MAP F1 ■ 35 N Great George St
■ 01 878 8547 ■ Open 10:30am–
4:30pm Tue–Sat ■ Adm
■ www.jamesjoyce.ie**

James Joyce *(see p42)* spent much of his early life north of the Liffey so it is a fitting area to house a museum dedicated to the Irish writer.

James Joyce Cultural Centre

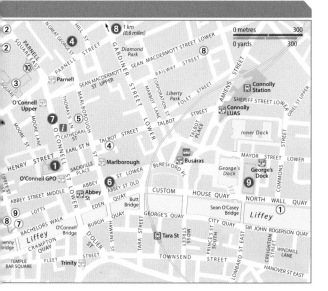

A Peasant Woman by Edgar Degas

5 Hugh Lane Gallery

MAP E1 ■ Charlemont House, Parnell Sq North ■ 01 222 5550 ■ Open 9:45am–6pm Tue–Thu, 9:45am–5pm Fri, 10am–5pm Sat, 11am–5pm Sun ■ www.hughlane.ie

Art-lover Hugh Lane spent his life collecting art, and today the permanent collection includes exceptional 19th- and 20th-century works by Irish and European artists, including Manet, Degas and Renoir. An addition is the Dublin-born painter Francis Bacon's studio.

NELSON'S PILLAR

In 1809, a controversial 40-m- (121-ft-) column topped with a 4-m- (13-ft-) statue of Nelson was erected in O'Connell Street. Several attempts were made over the years to destroy this symbol of British imperialism until, in 1966, a bomb damaged it so badly that it had to be dismantled.

6 Abbey Theatre

MAP F3 ■ 26 Lower Abbey St ■ 01 878 7222 ■ www.abbeytheatre.ie

The Irish National Theatre was founded at the Abbey Theatre *(see p48)* by the Gaelic Revival Movement led by Lady Augusta Gregory and W B Yeats *(see p42)* and first opened its doors in 1904. It had a radical reputation, putting on plays such as Sean O'Casey's *The Plough and the Stars*. The theatre then went into decline, before being gutted by fire in 1951. It reopened in 1966 with the Abbey stage, and its experimental annex, the Peacock stage.

7 O'Connell Street

MAP E2

One of the widest streets in Europe, O'Connell Street was designed by Luke Gardiner in the 1740s and was once lined with Classical buildings. Sadly, many of these were destroyed during the Easter Rising *(see p39)*. The Spire or "Monument of Light" *(see p41)* is a latter-day iconic hallmark.

Statue of nationalist leader, Daniel O'Connell on O'Connell Street

8 **Croke Park**
MAP T2 ■ Jones Rd ■ 01 819 2323 ■ Tours run daily (book ahead) ■ Adm ■ www.crokepark.ie

Croke Park has a special place in Dubliners' hearts as the home of Gaelic football and hurling, their national sports. A museum fills in the history, with an interactive games zone to test visitors' ball skills, but the big draw is the "skyline tour" on the stadium roof, where guides recount stories in front of wraparound views of city, sea and mountains.

Displays at EPIC Ireland

9 **EPIC Ireland**
MAP H3 ■ The CHQ Building, Custom House Quay ■ 01 906 0861 ■ Open 10am–5pm daily ■ Adm ■ www.epicchq.com

This popular attraction is set in the CHQ Building, an 1820s tea, spirits and tobacco warehouse. Twenty interactive galleries bring alive the story of Ireland's 10 million-strong diaspora, looking at why they left and where they ended up. There's also a state-of-the-art genealogy centre for those investigating their Irish roots.

10 **Jameson Distillery Bow Street**
MAP B3 ■ Bow St ■ 01 807 2355 ■ Open 10am–7pm (Fri & Sat: until 8pm) ■ Adm

Refurbished as a museum, the Jameson Distillery Bow Street, where whiskey was first made in the 1780s, offers a 40-minute tour that goes through the entire process of production of the Irish whiskey, from grain delivery to bottling. At the end of the tour there is a whiskey tasting.

A DAY'S STROLL AROUND THE NORTHSIDE

▶ **MORNING**

For breakfast in a lovely Georgian building head for **Cobalt Café** *(see p73)* on North Great George Street. Across the road, the **James Joyce Cultural Centre** *(see p69)* is worth a peep. Afterwards, stop by the **Gate Theatre** to book tickets for the evening's performance en route to **14 Henrietta Street** *(see p69)*, which peers into Dublin's past. Head back to Parnell Square to visit the **Hugh Lane Gallery** and view the art collection, before heading for lunch at the on-site café.

AFTERNOON

Cross stately **Parnell Square** *(see p69)* and head down **O'Connell Street** to take in the **GPO Building** *(see p68)*, perhaps devoting an hour to its striking Witness History exhibit. There's an optional pause for some retail therapy on neighbouring **Henry Street** *(MAP E2)*, one of the city's livelier shopping districts. Then continue south to the riverside, detouring to book for the **Abbey Theatre**, if you prefer the fare on offer there for the evening.

Stroll the riverside eastwards to **Custom House Quay**, then explore the riveting story of Irish migration at the **EPIC Ireland** attraction or aboard the **Jeanie Johnston** famine ship *(see p72)*. Wind down with a cocktail and a pretheatre meal at **Ely Bar & Grill** *(see p72)* or one of the other bars and restaurants in the CHQ building.

See map on pp68–9

The Best of the Rest

The Jeanie Johnston tall ship

1 The Jeanie Johnston
MAP H3 ▪ Custom House Quay ▪ 01 473 0111 ▪ Open 10am–4:30pm Mon–Fri (until 4pm Sat & Sun) ▪ Adm

This replica of the 1840s tall ship re-creates the squalid conditions endured by thousands of Irish voyaging to the New World.

2 Garden of Remembrance
MAP E1 ▪ Parnell Sq ▪ 01 821 3021 ▪ Open 9:30am–6pm (until dusk in winter)

Opened in 1966, this peaceful park commemorates all those who died in the fight for Irish Freedom.

3 Rotunda Hospital
MAP E1 ▪ Parnell Sq

The first purpose-built maternity hospital in Europe in 1745. Inside there is a beautiful late-Baroque chapel.

4 Decorative Arts and History Museum
MAP A3 ▪ Collins Barracks, Bernurb St ▪ Open 10am–5pm Tue–Sat, 1–5pm Sun & Mon

Exhibits (see pp14–15) include Soldiers and Chiefs (military history), The Way We Wore (fashion) and Irish silver.

5 St Mary's Pro Cathedral
MAP F2 ▪ 83 Marlborough St ▪ 01 874 5441 ▪ Open 8am–5pm Mon–Fri; 9am–7pm Sat; 9am–1pm & 5–7pm Sun

Since 1825, St Mary's has been playing the part of a cathedral in Catholic Dublin. It is home to the renowned Palestrina choir, who sing the Sunday morning service.

6 King's Inns
MAP C1 ▪ Henrietta St, Constitution Hill ▪ 01 874 4630 ▪ Grounds only (open to the public)

Fine Georgian buildings, designed by James Gandon in the 1790s as a training school for barristers.

7 Smithfield
MAP B3

This redeveloped cobbled area, is home to horse fairs, which are held biannually. It is also used for concerts.

8 North Inner City Folklore Project
MAP D3 ▪ Railway St ▪ 01 547 6188 ▪ Open 2–4pm Tue–Sat ▪ www.folkloreproject.ie

This treasure trove of memorabilia offers a gritty insight into life in Dublin's former tenement slums.

9 St Michan's Church
MAP C3 ▪ Church St ▪ 01 872 4154 ▪ Open 10am–12:30pm & 2–4pm Mon–Fri, 10am–12:30pm Sat ▪ Adm

The attraction at this ancient church is the macabre mummified bodies.

10 Gate Theatre
MAP E1 ▪ Parnell Sq ▪ 01 874 4045 ▪ www.gatetheatre.ie

Converted from the Assembly Rooms, this (see p48) was known for high-class European productions, and today it stages both new plays and classics.

Façade of the Gate Theatre

Places to Eat

PRICE CATEGORIES
For a three-course meal for one with half a bottle of wine (or equivalent meal), taxes and extra charges.
....
€ under €45 ■ €€ €45–€90 ■ €€€ over €90

1 Mr Fox
MAP H2 ■ 38 Parnell Sq ■ 01 874 7778 ■ www.mrfox.ie ■ €€€
Set in the basement of a beautiful Georgian building, Mr Fox offers a set menu of fine-dining dishes, with an Irish twist.

2 Chapter One
MAP E1 ■ 18–19 Parnell Sq ■ 01 873 2266 ■ Closed Mon & Sun ■ www.chapteronerestaurant.com ■ €€€
Led by Mickael Viljanen, Chapter One is a recipient of two Michelin stars and one of Dublin's best restaurants (see p53). Try the excellent "pre-theatre" dinner menu with Irish and French cuisine. Advance booking required.

3 Han Sung
MAP E1 ■ 22 Strand St Great ■ 01 559 0503 ■ www.hansung dublin.com ■ €
Situated at the back of an Asian supermarket, this casual canteen serves delicious Korean food such as *bibimbap* (rice topped with veggies) and *japchae* (stir-fried glass noodles).

4 101 Talbot Street
MAP F2 ■ 101–2 Talbot St ■ 01 874 5011 ■ Closed Sun & Mon ■ www.101talbot.ie ■ €€
Just around the corner from the Abbey Theatre, try curries and traditional classics with a modern twist (see p52). A vegetarian menu is also available.

5 Panem
MAP E3 ■ 21 Lower Ormond Quay ■ 01 872 8510 ■ www.panem.ie ■ €
Take gorgeous filled focaccias and croissants out on to the boardwalk in the summer, or instead enjoy the chic interiors of this tiny restaurant.

6 Ristorante Romano
MAP D3 ■ 12 Capel St ■ 01 872 6868 ■ Closed Sun ■ €
Traditional Ristorante Romano serves Italian cuisine and handmade pasta. Expect hearty portions and a lovely cosy atmosphere.

7 The Woollen Mills
MAP E3 ■ 42 Lower Ormond Quay ■ 01 828 0835 ■ €€
This café's versatile menu spans full Irish breakfast to mains and cocktails. Try the fishcakes with bok choy.

Fine Irish cuisine at the Winding Stair

8 The Winding Stair
MAP E3 ■ 40 Lower Ormond Quay ■ 01 872 7320 ■ www.winding-stair.com ■ €€
A simple place, set above a bookshop, offering the best of Irish produce; do not miss the potted crab.

9 The Lotts Café Bar
MAP E3 ■ 9 Lower Liffey St ■ 01 872 7669 ■ www.thelottscafe bar.com ■ €
This antique spot serves Irish steaks sizzled on a stone at your table.

10 PHX Bistro
MAP B3 ■ 12 Ellis Quay ■ 01 611 1161 ■ www.phxbistro.com ■ €
A riverside restaurant serving Irish cuisine with a twist. Try the spicy chicken wings with Cashel cheese.

See map on pp68–9

TOP 10 Greater Dublin

The area around Dublin's city centre is rich with attractions, from stunning country estates – survivors of the Georgian heyday – to ancient Celtic remains and some spectacular scenery and walks, both in landscaped surroundings and wilder natural settings. As in days gone by, many of Ireland's wealthy choose to live in County Dublin's peaceful villages, benefiting from their close proximity to the capital while enjoying a more traditional way of life. The ten sights selected here are all less than an hour's drive from Dublin.

Ship in a bottle, Maritime Museum

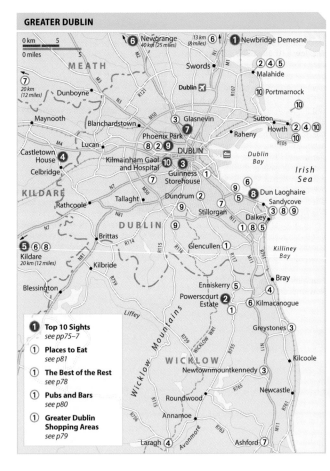

GREATER DUBLIN

0 km   5
0 miles   5

MEATH

Newgrange
40 km (25 miles)   13 km
(8 miles)

Swords

Dunboyne
20 km
(12 miles)

Maynooth

Blanchardstown

Phoenix Park

Lucan

Castletown
House

Celbridge

KILDARE

Rathcoole

Tallaght

Brittas

Kildare
20 km (12 miles)

Kilbride

Blessington

Kilmainham Gaol
and Hospital

Dublin ✈

Glasnevin

DUBLIN

Guinness
Storehouse

Dundrum

Stillorgan

DUBLIN

Glencullen

Enniskerry

Powerscourt
Estate

Liffey

Newbridge Demesne

Malahide

Portmarnock

Sutton

Howth

Raheny

Dublin
Bay

Irish
Sea

Dun Laoghaire

Sandycove

Dalkey

Killiney
Bay

Bray

Kilmacanogue

Greystones

Kilcoole

Newcastle

WICKLOW
Mountains

WICKLOW

Newtownmountkennedy

Roundwood

Annamoe

Laragh   Avonmore   Ashford

- ① **Top 10 Sights**
  see pp75–7
- ① **Places to Eat**
  see p81
- ① **The Best of the Rest**
  see p78
- ① **Pubs and Bars**
  see p80
- ① **Greater Dublin Shopping Areas**
  see p79

1 Newbridge Demesne

MAP U1 ■ Donabate ■ 01 843 6534 ■ House and farm: open hours vary, check website ■ Adm ■ www.newbridgehouseandfarm.com

A must for architecture fans, this attractive house lies north of Dublin at the seaside village of Donabate. The house was initially designed for Archbishop Charles Cobbe in 1737 by George Semple – the Cobbe family still live in the upper half of the house although the council bought it from them in the 1980s. Rooms include the beautifully preserved Red Drawing Room, the huge kitchen and the Museum of Curiosities.

2 Powerscourt Estate

MAP T3 ■ Enniskerry, Co Wicklow ■ 01 204 6000 ■ Open hours vary, check website ■ Adm ■ www.powerscourt.com

Five minutes from the pretty village of Enniskerry, reached via bus from Dublin, Powerscourt Estate makes a great day trip. Visitors approach the house down a long beech-lined avenue with beautiful views across the valley. The house, designed by Richard Cassels in the 1730s, was gutted by fire in 1974, but a small exhibition gives the "before and after" story of its reconstruction. The main part of the house is now an up-market shop (see p79) and large restaurant. The gardens are spread over a steep slope and steps lead down to a lake.

Display at the Guinness Storehouse

3 Guinness Storehouse

To the west of the centre, this comprehensive exhibition (see pp30–31), set in the old brewery building, takes the visitor through the creation of the famous beer, from the grain to the glass of creamy-topped liquid.

4 Castletown House

MAP N5 ■ Celbridge, Co Kildare ■ 01 628 8252 ■ Open mid-Mar–Oct: 10am–4pm daily ■ Adm ■ www.castletown.ie

As the first example of Palladianism in Ireland (1722–9), it maintains its significance in the country. Architects Alessandro Galilei and Sir Edward Lovett Pearce built the house for William Conolly, Speaker of the Irish Parliament. The interiors were commissioned by Lady Louisa Lennox, wife of Conolly's great-nephew Tom, who moved here in 1758. The house remained in the family until 1965. Its beautiful grounds are open to visitors.

Panoramic views from Powerscourt Estate

The enchanting Japanese Gardens at the National Stud

5 National Stud

MAP N5 ▪ Kildare ▪ 045 521 617 ▪ Open Feb–late Dec: 10am–6pm daily (Nov & Dec: until 4pm) ▪ Adm ▪ www.irishnationalstud.ie

Visitors can tour this state-run bloodstock farm to learn about the breeding and training of these fine racehorses. The museum charts the development of the stud since its establishment by Colonel Hall Walker in 1900. Also within the estate are the Japanese Gardens, laid out between 1906 and 1910 by Hall Walker and two Japanese gardeners to represent the "life of man". St Fiachra's Garden was created to mark the Millennium and was named after a 6th-century monk with a love of gardening.

6 Newgrange and the Boyne Valley

MAP M5 ▪ Boyne Valley ▪ 041 988 0300 ▪ Open 9:30am–5pm daily (open hours vary, call ahead to check) ▪ Adm ▪ www.heritageireland.ie

Newgrange is one of the most significant passage graves in Europe (see p38). Its origins are shrouded in mystery. Built by Stone Age farmers, the circular mound contains a passage, which leads into a chamber. Visitors must pass through the excellent Brú na Bóinne Visitor Centre and join a tour. Anyone with an interest in archaeology will find the Boyne Valley fascinating, especially the ancient Hills of Tara and Slane, which feature in Celtic mythology.

Glasshouse, National Botanic Gardens

7 Glasnevin Cemetery and National Botanic Gardens

MAP T2 ▪ Glasnevin Cemetery: Finglas Rd; 01 882 6550; open 10am–5pm daily; adm for museum and tours; www.glasnevintrust.ie ▪ National Botanic Gardens: Botanic Rd; 01 804 0300; open Mar–Sep: 9am–5pm Mon–Fri, 10am–6pm Sat & Sun (winter: until 4:40pm daily); www.botanicgardens.ie

Those interred here include Michael Collins, Christy Brown and Maud Gonne. Next to the cemetery are the fine National Botanic Gardens.

ANCIENT OBSERVATORY

When archaeologists decided to restore Newgrange to as close to its original state as possible, they discovered that on the dawn of the winter solstice (21 December) sunlight beams through the roof on to the burial chamber, proving it to be the earliest known solar observatory.

8 National Maritime Museum

MAP U2 ■ Haigh Terrace, Dun Laoghaire ■ 01 280 0969 ■ Open 11am–5pm daily ■ Adm ■ www.mariner.ie

Inspiringly arranged inside the atmospheric 180-year-old Mariners Church at Dun Laoghaire docks, this magnificent collection of engines, instruments, models and charts was revamped in 2012, and tells the story of a nation at sea. Enthusiastic and highly knowledgeable guides bring to life the history of maritime navigation, exploration, discoveries and disasters down the ages. There are also exhibits dedicated to the ill-fated *Titanic* and the *Great Eastern*, once the world's largest ship. You could end your visit at the excellent maritime-themed shop.

9 Phoenix Park

There is enough to see within this vast park *(see pp34–5)* to keep the visitor busy for a whole day. The zoo, with its elephants, is one of the main attractions, and Áras an Uachtaráin provides the official home to the President of Ireland.

10 Kilmainham Gaol and Hospital

At the far west of the city, these two institutions *(see pp32–3)* could not be more different. The forbidding Kilmainham Gaol, with its grim history, was restored and opened as a museum in the 1960s. In contrast, the former hospital is a fine and beautiful building, restored in the 1980s and is now home to the spectacular Irish Museum of Modern Art.

Kilmainham Hospital

A DRIVE AROUND GREATER DUBLIN

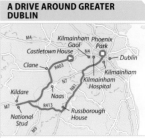

▶ **MORNING**

Head out of Dublin on the N4 west road to Celbridge and visit **Castletown House** *(see p75)*. Take the first tour and you will get an excellent history of the house and family, as well as being talked through the architectural high-lights. Negotiate your way back to the Naas Road (N7) via Clane, across the Curragh towards Kildare and the **National Stud** – there's an excellent café here for a coffee. After a leisurely wander around the gardens, you could take the fascinating and very informative tour through the business of bloodstock.

After leaving Kildare head for **Russborough House** *(see p85)* by returning to Naas and taking the N81 Blessington road. The café-at Russborough House serves simple but delicious homemade fare for lunch. After lunch, tour the house and savour the wonderful views of the **Wicklow Mountains**.

AFTERNOON

Head back to Dublin and follow signs for **Kilmainham Gaol**. After a somewhat sombre visit to this former prison, cut across to **Kilmainham Hospital** for the impressive Irish Museum of Modern Art. If further refreshment is required after your visit, go to the Kemp Sisters' Gallery Café in the basement. Standing in the formal gardens here, you get a great view across to the huge expanse of **Phoenix Park**, which you could make a visit to on your way back into the centre, energy levels permitting.

See map on p74 ⟵

The Best of the Rest

① Dalkey Castle and Heritage Centre

MAP U3 ■ 01 285 8366 ■ Castle St, Dalkey ■ Open 10am–5:30pm Wed–Mon (from 11am Sat & Sun) ■ www.dalkeycastle.com

Dalkey's history is brought to life amid the castle ruins. You can enjoy lovely views from the battlements.

② Howth

MAP U2

This busy fishing port offers great walks around the headland. Look out for seals when the boats come in.

③ James Joyce Tower and Museum

MAP U2 ■ Sandycove ■ 01 280 9265 ■ Open 10am–4pm Wed–Sun ■ www.joycetower.ie

The first chapter of *Ulysses* (see p42) was set here and a museum contains Joyce memorabilia.

④ Killruddery House

MAP U3 ■ Bray ■ 01 286 3405 ■ Open hours vary, check website ■ Adm ■ www.killruddery.com

Home to the Earls of Meath, the formal gardens are the main attraction of this grand estate.

⑤ Malahide Castle

MAP U1 ■ Malahide ■ 01 816 9538 ■ Open daily ■ Adm

With five ghosts and rounded towers, this castle has a fairy tale quality.

⑥ Skerries Mills

MAP M6 ■ Skerries ■ 01 849 5208 ■ Open 10am–5:30pm (winter: until 4:30pm) ■ Adm ■ www.skerriesmills.ie

This seaside enclave has been stone-grinding flour for at least 500 years, and its windmills and water-mill make an enlightening day out.

⑦ Drimnagh Castle

MAP T2 ■ Long Mile Rd, Dublin 12 ■ 01 450 2530 ■ Tours: 10am–3pm Mon–Thu (until noon Fri) ■ Adm ■ www.drimnaghcastle.org

The only Irish castle still hemmed by a flooded moat, it has a restored great hall and 17th-century gardens.

⑧ Killiney Hill Park

MAP U3 ■ Co Dublin

It is worth the climb here for the spectacular views over Dublin Bay.

⑨ St Enda's Park

MAP T2 ■ Grange Rd, Rathfarnham ■ 01 493 4208

One of Dublin's more charming parks, with riverside walks, follies, a waterfall and walled garden.

⑩ Ireland's Eye

MAP U2 ■ Island Ferries, Howth ■ 086 645 9154 ■ www.islandferries.net

Tour this small uninhabited island by boat from Howth to spot its colony of seals, seabirds and puffins up close.

Malahide Castle set in a lush garden

Greater Dublin Shopping Areas

 Powerscourt
MAP T3 ■ Powerscourt
House, Enniskerry
Spread over two floors of the
main house *(see p75)* are numerous
different outlets. Avoca is the main
retailer but there are plenty of
others, including The Design Loft
and Global Village interiors. The
garden centre is also excellent.

Dundrum Town Centre shops

 Dundrum Town Centre
MAP T2 ■ Dundrum
Said to be Ireland's largest shopping
centre, the massive Dundrum Centre
has over 160 shops, including Harvey
Nichols, Penneys and Hobbs, as well
as a cinema, restaurants, a theatre
and a rainforest style mini golf course.

**3 Fishers of
Newtownmountkennedy**
MAP U4 ■ The Old Schoolhouse,
Newtownmountkennedy ■ 01 281
9404 ■ www.fishers.ie
Tucked away in a rather unlikely
spot is this family-run place, selling
up-market women's fashions and
traditional men's country clothes.

4 Malahide
MAP U1
An extremely attractive village with
its streets arranged in a cross-grid
pattern. There are a variety of shops

to visit, including an excellent wine
shop, designer boutiques and a
well-stocked hardware store.

5 Dalkey
MAP U3
Another pretty seaside village,
and the home of many international
stars. There are a couple of excellent
galleries as well as designer boutiques selling pure linen clothes
and original silk knitwear.

6 Avoca Handweavers

MAP U3 ■ Kilmacanogue,
Co Wicklow ■ 01 274 6900
■ www.avoca.ie
This beautiful Avoca store stocks
a wide range of own-label Irish-
made clothes, gifts and foods.
The self-serve café sells huge
helpings of Mediterranean food.

7 Mount Usher Gardens

MAP U5 ■ Ashford
The arcade of shops here includes
homewares, equestrian clothes
and equipments, and an art gallery.

8 Kildare Village
MAP N5 ■ Nurney Rd, Kildare
town ■ 045 520 501
This outlet shopping centre sells
discounted designer brands. There
are plenty of nice cafés if you need a
break from the shops and an express
bus runs from Dublin Airport.

**9 Glasthule and
Sandycove**
MAP U2
These two pretty seaside villages sit
alongside each other and are packed
with boutiques and food sellers.
Caviston's Food Emporium on
Glasthule Road is a real delight.

10 Wrights of Howth
MAP U2 ■ 14 West Pier, Howth
■ 01 816 7347
Right on the pier, Wrights has a great
selection of fresh and smoked fish, as
well as luxury seafood gift hampers.

See map on p74

Pubs and Bars

Atmospheric Johnnie Fox's pub

1 Johnnie Fox's
MAP T3 ■ Glencullen ■ 01 295 5647 ■ www.jfp.ie

Well-known Johnnie Fox's is, 5 km (3 miles) from Enniskerry. The 18th-century inn is full of old beams and roaring open fires, and has a seemingly endless series of rooms.

2 Wrights Anglers Rest
MAP S2 ■ Strawberry Beds ■ 01 820 4351 ■ www.theanglersrest.ie

Featuring a lovely outdoor patio in summer and an open fire in winter, this cosy pub serves a range of beers and wines, along with great food.

3 John Kavanagh
MAP T2 ■ 1 Prospect Sq, Dublin 9 ■ 08 7296 3713

Well placed for a bite while visiting Glasnevin Cemetery and the National Botanic Gardens (see p76) this old-school pub dating from 1833 is also known as Gravediggers.

4 Lynhams Laragh Inn
MAP T5 ■ Laragh, Co Wicklow ■ 0404 45345 ■ www.lynhamsof laragh.ie

Just east of Glendalough, is a welcoming pub with hearty fires and a jolly crowd of locals.

5 The Purty Kitchen
MAP U2 ■ 3–5 Old Dunleary Rd, Dun Laoghaire ■ 01 284 3576 ■ www.purtykitchen.com

Top-notch seafood within a stone's throw of the Dun Laoghaire seafront.

6 The Silken Thomas
MAP N5 ■ The Sq, Kildare ■ 045 522 232 ■ Restaurant: open daily

This pub and restaurant produce excellent and reasonably priced bar food. It is named after the fancy attire worn by Thomas Fitzgerald (see p18), famous for his rebellion against King Henry VIII in the mid-16th century.

7 James Griffin Pub
MAP M5 ■ High St, Trim, Co Meath ■ 046 943 1295

An award-winning traditional pub in the pretty town of Trim. The lively atmosphere makes this an ideal place to go to after a visit to the Trim Castle. There is regular live Irish music.

8 Ryan's & FX Buckley
MAP T2 ■ 28 Parkgate St, Dublin 8 ■ 01 671 9352 ■ www.fx buckley.ie

The dining room above Ryan's pub (see p50) serves excellent steak, which is cooked to perfection in a charcoal oven.

9 The Merry Ploughboy Pub
MAP T3 ■ Rockbrook, Edmondstown Rd, Rathfarnham ■ www.mpbpub.com

If you're looking forward to traditional Irish music, song and dance, head to Rathfarnham, near the Dublin mountains, for a night of Irish charm.

10 Abbey Tavern
MAP U2 ■ 28 Abbey St, Howth ■ 01 839 0307 ■ www.abbeytavern.ie

There's a great atmosphere in this 16th-century inn, which makes the most of its antique features. It hosts regular traditional Irish evenings.

Places to Eat

1 **Mulberry Garden**
MAP T2 ■ Mulberry Lane
■ 01 269 3300 ■ Closed Sun–Tue
■ www.mulberrygarden.ie ■ €€€

Tucked away in a quaint cottage in Donnybrook, this place *(see p52)* champions a seasonal menu which is paired with an extensive wine list.

2 **Bon Appetit**
MAP U1 ■ 9 James Terrace,
Malahide ■ 01 845 0314 ■ €€

An inviting and lively restaurant, Bon Appetit offers creative dishes. The early and late bird menus offer great value for money.

3 **Hungry Monk**
MAP U4 ■ Church Rd, Greystones
■ 01 287 5759 ■ Closed Mon & Tue
■ €€

This quirky restaurant offers game in winter and fish dishes in summer.

King Sitric overlooking the sea

4 **King Sitric**
MAP U2 ■ East Pier, Howth,
Co Dublin ■ 01 832 5235 ■ €€

This seaside restaurant *(see p131)* serves fresh local seafood. You can choose to dine in its cosy interiors, on the outdoor terrace or in a beach hut.

5 **Poppies**
MAP T3 ■ The Sq, Enniskerry
■ 01 282 8869 ■ €

With cottage-style interiors matching an English tearoom, Poppies generously serves home-cooked food.

PRICE CATEGORIES
For a three-course meal for one with half a bottle of wine (or equivalent meal), taxes and extra charges.

€ under €45   €€ €45–€90   €€€ over €90

6 **Hartley's**
MAP U2 ■ 1 Harbour Rd,
Dun Laoghaire ■ 01 280 6767
■ Closed Mon & Tue ■ €

Set in a building that used to be the Customs Hall, this special restaurant offers lots of space and light, with high ceilings and attractive decor. The seafood menu is delicious.

7 **Riba**
MAP T2 ■ 4 Lower Kilmacud
Rd, Stillorgan ■ 01 288 1999
■ Closed Tue ■ €€

This smart bistro serves spicy chicken wings, dry-aged sirloins, salads and a great burger with smoked cheese.

8 **Cavistons**
MAP U2 ■ 59 Glasthule Rd,
Sandycove ■ 01 280 9120 ■ Closed
Mon & Sun ■ €€

This smart seafood restaurant has a reputation for producing mouth-watering fish dishes. Book in advance for lunch or dinner sittings.

9 **Liath**
MAP T2 ■ 19a Main St,
Blackrock ■ 01 212 3676 ■ Closed
Wed–Sat L; Sun–Tue ■ www.liath
restaurant.com ■ €€€

Book well in advance (online bookings only), at this tiny restaurant, for the "no choices" set dinner menu of 'new Irish' cuisine.

10 **The Seaview**
MAP U1 ■ Portmarnock
Hotel and Golf Links, Strand Rd,
Portmarnock ■ 01 846 0611 ■ €€

Housed in a hotel, this restaurant offers hearty Irish fare along with stunning views of Ireland's Eye. Try the Dublin Bay seafood chowder and the crab sandwich.

See map on p74

TOP 10 **Wicklow Mountains**

The rugged beauty of the Wicklow Mountains, seen from Wicklow Gap

① **Wicklow Gap**
MAP S5

This atmospheric spot is on the R756 road. From here, it's a boggy hike up to the 817-m- (2,680-ft-) Tonelagee viewpoint. Take in breathtaking views of the lonely beauty of the Wicklow Mountains. Another worthwhile stop is the Sally Gap, a remote crossroads on the R115 road. In times past, its bogs were a favourite hideout for Irish warriors and rebels.

Glendalough monastic site

② **Glendalough**
MAP S5 ▪ County Wicklow ▪ 040 445 325 ▪ Open daily (call ahead for open hours)

A large part of the charm of this important monastic site is its location.

The name translates as "the valley of the two lakes". The Upper Lake provides splendid scenery, with wooded slopes and a plunging waterfall, while the Lower Lake is surrounded by monastic ruins. St Kevin, a member of the Leinster royal family, founded the monastery in the 6th century and it became a renowned centre of Celtic learning.

③ **Wicklow Way**
MAP S5

For visitors who really want to see the mountains at close hand, there's nothing better than walking. Numerous easy, marked local paths run through the pretty hill country, while the Wicklow Way is more demanding and for serious hikers. This 127-km (79-mile) marked path, taking around 9 days, makes its way through the heart of the region, all the way from Dublin to Clonegal, in County Carlow.

④ **Clara Lara Fun Park**
MAP T5 ▪ Open May: Sat & Sun; Jun–Aug: daily

A top recreation site for families, the Fun Park is in the Vale of Clara, and near the village of Laragh – hence the name. Most of the rides are water-based such as canoeing, but there are Go Karts too. Here is the highest slide in Ireland, as well as tree-houses, climbing frames and picnic areas.

Previous pages The Giant's Causeway, Northern Ireland

⑤ Avondale Forest Park

MAP T6 ■ Rathdrum ■ 040 446 111 ■ Open Apr–Sep: Thu–Sun ■ Adm

Charles Stewart Parnell *(see p39)* was born in Georgian Avondale House, which is now a museum to his memory. Beautiful Avondale Forest Park has waymarked trails, and also features Beyond the Trees, a treetop walk that has a 38-m- (125-ft-) high viewing tower.

⑥ Devil's Glen

MAP U5

Although close to Wicklow Town, this romantic wooded glen, with its waterfall and chirruping birds, is a haven of peace and tranquillity. It is part of the pretty valley of the Vartry. Perfect for walking or riding, it makes a quiet escape within an hour's drive of Dublin. There are many pleasant self-catering apartments and small cottages to rent, as well as stables and other facilities.

⑦ Wicklow Town

MAP U5 ■ Wicklow Gaol: open mid-Apr–Sep: 10am–6pm daily; adm; www.wicklowshistoricgaol.com

Wicklow's modest county town has a low-key charm, with its harbour and unpretentious pubs. The one unmissable sight is Wicklow Gaol. Hundreds of Irish rebels were detained here, often tortured and, in many cases, hanged. Evocative exhibitions fill in the background, and include a section on the deportation of the inmates to colonies, such as Australia.

The charming marina at Wicklow Town

⑧ Russborough House

MAP N5 ■ Open 10am–6pm ■ Adm ■ www.russborough.ie

Russborough House holds the famous Beit Art Collection. Nearby, the River Liffey has been dammed to form a picturesque reservoir.

Mount Usher Gardens, Ashford

⑨ Mount Usher Gardens

MAP U5 ■ Ashford ■ Open 10am–6pm daily ■ Adm ■ www.mountusher gardens.ie

Set in a sheltered valley at Ashford, northwest of Wicklow town, these fine "Robinsonian" gardens combine a distinguished collection of trees and shrubs as well as informal floral planting. A tree trail guide directs visitors to the show-stoppers.

⑩ Vale of Avoca

MAP T6

"There is not in the wide world a valley so sweet," wrote 19th-century poet Thomas Moore in his work *The Meeting of the Waters,* capturing the beauty of this gentle valley. It is perhaps not quite as idyllic now as it was then, but the meeting of rust-coloured rivers among wooded hills is still enticing. Avoca Handweavers *(see p79),* at the nearby village, produces tweeds in the oldest handweaving mill in Ireland, that has been in operation since 1723.

🔟 Around Waterford

Green and hilly County Waterford is exposed to the Atlantic to the south, the beautiful Blackwater and Suir rivers penetrate far inland, while Waterford City stands by an excellent natural harbour. All these factors made this corner of the southeast almost too welcoming to outsiders – Waterford City (Vadrafjord in Norse), founded in 853 CE, is thought to be the oldest surviving Viking town in Europe. Later, Normans also chose this spot for their first Irish settlement. In few other places can Celtic, Norse and Norman relics be found so close to one another. In modern times, Waterford has been staunchly patriotic and proud of its heritage – it even has a small *Gaeltacht* (Irish-speaking district) around the village of Rinn.

The fishing village of Dunmore East

1 Dunmore East
MAP Q5

A working fishing harbour with brightly coloured boats, and little cottages set among woods, this attractive village has some excellent seafood restaurants and traditional pubs and is a favourite outing for a drink, lunch or a waterfront stroll. Many of the cottages are available for holiday lets. Nearby sandy coves include the popular Lady's Cove beach, and there are several enjoyable marked walks and hikes.

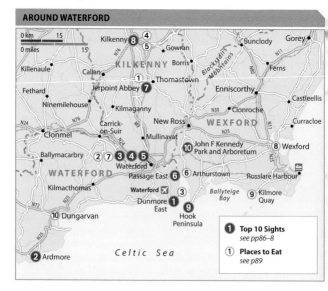

AROUND WATERFORD

Top 10 Sights
see pp86–8

Places to Eat
see p89

The sweeping sandy bay at Ardmore

2 Ardmore
MAP Q4

Pretty Ardmore is a popular little beach resort. The hill behind is the site of St Declan's 5th-century monastery, probably the oldest in Ireland. Its many evocative remains (mostly dating from the 12th century) include St Declan's Cathedral, a fine example of a high cross, and a 30-m (100-ft) round tower.

3 House of Waterford Crystal

MAP Q5 ■ The Mall, Waterford City ■ 05 131 7000 ■ Open hours vary, check website ■ Adm for tour ■ www.waterfordvisitorcentre.com

The Waterford Crystal factory, for many years a major source of employment and local pride, is now located in a grand old building which used to house the electricity board. About 53,000 pieces are created here annually by specialist glassblowers and cutters. Tours of the factory are available, and there is a retail store and a café.

4 Waterford City Centre
MAP Q5

Surviving sections of Waterford's city walls show clearly the limits of the original Viking settlement, also bordered on one side by the River Suir. Today, that waterfront, with its lively and attractive quays, is the focal point of the town. The 18th-century City Hall houses important local memorabilia The city is famous for its glassworks.

5 Waterford Treasures
MAP Q5 ■ Waterford ■ 051 849 501 ■ Open hours vary, check website ■ Adm ■ www.waterford treasures.com

These five museums, located in Waterford city, document over 1,000 years of history. Reginald's Tower houses the Treasures of Viking Waterford and an exhibition on medieval Waterford is displayed in Chorister's Hall. The Georgian era is represented in the former Bishop's Palace. The Museum of Time and the Museum of Silver were opened in 2021.

6 Passage East
MAP Q5

A small, enjoyable ferry plies back and forth across Waterford Harbour from this peaceful, scenic waterside village. It was at this spot that the Normans arrived in Ireland in 1170 and their sturdy stone tower still stands guard over the harbour.

The harbour at Passage East

Stone carvings in Jerpoint Abbey

7 Jerpoint Abbey

MAP P5 ■ Thomastown
■ 05 6772 4623 ■ Open Mar–Nov: 9am–4pm daily (last adm 3:15pm) ■ Adm

One of Ireland's best examples of a Cistercian monastery, the restored chapterhouse and part of the cloisters of 12th-century Jerpoint stand grandly among its ruins in a peaceful countryside setting. The Jerpoint community established itself as a centre of culture and learning, and was very prosperous until the Dissolution in 1540, when it was surrendered to the Crown. Many fine pieces of stone-carving can be seen, and there is a useful Interpretative Centre.

8 Kilkenny

MAP P4

Ireland's medieval capital, Kilkenny is undoubtedly Ireland's loveliest inland city. It has rapidly emerged as a food capital, thanks to the clutch of creative restaurants, some of which are Michelin-starred. Its Norman castle looms impressively over the River Nore, and the old stable block has been converted into a hub for Irish arts and crafts.

MEDIEVAL KILKENNY

The first medieval city of Ireland, Kilkenny celebrated its heritage along its 'Medieval Mile' – with sights such as the Black Abbey and St Canice's Cathedral as well as the Medieval Mile Museum, located in a 12th-century converted church. The medieval ruins of Kells Priory once housed the *Book of Kells*.

The city's rewarding medieval remnants include St Canice's Cathedral and late 16th-century Rothe House, with a genealogy centre, gardens and a museum, containing a number of archaeological artifacts.

9 Hook Peninsula

MAP Q5 ■ Tintern Abbey: open Apr–Oct: 10am–5pm; adm

The peaceful "Ring of Hook" headland lies beside the broad Waterford Harbour, with long sandy beaches, rugged cliffs and many relics of the past. At the northeast corner, ruined Tintern Abbey – with its beautiful grounds and riverside setting – was founded in 1200 and, although much altered and restored, remains atmospheric. The peninsula's wild tip, where there has been a lighthouse since the 5th century, is beloved of bird-watchers.

Partially restored Tintern Abbey

10 John F Kennedy Park and Arboretum

MAP P5 ■ New Ross ■ Open 10am–dusk daily ■ Adm

Some 4,500 international species of trees and shrubs – all carefully labelled – grow in this delightful 620 acre (252 ha) arboretum, created in memory of the former US president. You can visit the Kennedy Homestead in New Ross and see the birthplace of his great-grandfather.

Places to Eat

 Lady Helen Restaurant
MAP P5 ■ Mount Juliet,
Thomastown ■ 056 777 3000
■ Closed Mon & Sun ■ €€€

This sophisticated restaurant offers an imaginative menu with international influences. It has one Michelin star and four AA rosettes.

2 **Bianconi**
MAP Q5 ■ Granville Hotel,
Waterford ■ 051 305555 ■ Closed
Mon–Sat L ■ €€

Housed in a hotel overlooking the quayside, this award-winning restaurant serves the best of contemporary, Italian-influenced cuisine.

3 **The Spinnaker**
MAP Q5 ■ Dunmore East
■ 051 383133 ■ €

Award-winning nautical-themed bar and beer garden, The Spinnaker serves delicious seafood dishes.

4 **Rinuccini**
MAP P4 ■ 1 The Parade,
Kilkenny ■ 056 776 1575 ■ €€

This award-winning family-run restaurant serves classic Italian and Irish dishes in a sophisticated setting.

5 **Campagne**
MAP P4 ■ Gas House Lane,
Kilkenny ■ 056 777 2858 ■ Closed
Mon–Thu L; Sun–Tue D ■ €€

Michelin-starred chef-patron Garrett Byrne fuses French and Irish influences. Try the roast brill with seaweed butter sauce.

Campagne's cool, art-filled interior

PRICE CATEGORIES
For a three-course meal for one with half a bottle of wine (or equivalent meal), taxes and extra charges.
....
€ under €45   €€ €45–€90   €€€ over €90

6 **The Harvest Room at Dunbrody Country House**
MAP P5 ■ Arthurstown ■ 051 389600
■ Closed Wed–Sat L; Mon & Tue ■ €€

Owner and chef Kevin Dundon is one of Ireland's finest cooks. The Harvest Room serves outstanding food and has an excellent wine list. Booking in advance is essential.

7 **McLeary's Restaurant**
MAP Q5 ■ 122 Parade Quay,
Waterford ■ 051 853444 ■ Closed
Mon & Sun ■ €€

This friendly steakhouse also serves seafood such as crispy calamari and traditional fish and chips. It has a café on the other side of the city.

8 **Greenacres Bistro**
MAP P5 ■ Selskar, Wexford
■ 053 912 2975 ■ Closed Mon & Sun
■ €€

An attractive restaurant with a shop and an art gallery, this bistro is popular for its modern Irish fare, artisanal cheeses and its exceptional wine list.

9 **The Little Saltee**
MAP Q5 ■ Kilmore Quay
■ 053 912 9911 ■ Closed Mon & Tue
(winter: Mon–Thu) ■ €

A popular harbourside restaurant, "Saltee's Chipper" serves great fish and chips. It also offers takeaway to enjoy on the beach.

10 **The Tannery**
MAP Q4 ■ 10 Quay St,
Dungarvan ■ 058 45420 ■ Closed L;
Mon ■ €€€

Don't miss out on chef Paul Flynn's award-winning modern Irish cuisine. There is also a cookery school here. For a more affordable option, try the selection at the wine bar.

See map on p86

TOP10 The Ring of Kerry and the Dingle Peninsula

The southwest of Ireland is one of the most beautiful regions of the country. The Killarney National Park is an experience in itself but, if at all possible, like the Ring of Kerry, it should be visited off-season – the area has become so popular that driving the Ring can turn into a nightmare of tour buses in high season. The area is largely made up of peninsulas: the stunning Dingle Peninsula to the north, Iveragh which is located centrally, and is the largest; and the Beara Peninsula which offers dramatic views from its two impressive mountain ranges that run along its spine. Amid this landscape are some striking Georgian residences, pretty villages and ancient religious sites.

Puffins on Skellig Michael

1 Valentia Island and the Skelligs

MAP Q1 ■ Co Kerry

The Skellig Experience visitor centre, near the causeway, links Valentia Island to the mainland. It includes exhibits on the history of the Skellig

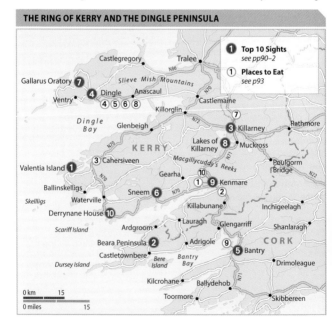

THE RING OF KERRY AND THE DINGLE PENINSULA

| Top 10 Sights | 1 | see pp90–2 |
| Places to Eat | 1 | see p93 |

Fishing boats in the fine natural harbour at Dingle

Michael monastic site and a range of information on local flora and fauna. Valentia is a popular holiday spot and is particularly good for watersports, but now the only inhabitants of the Skelligs are the birds. Cruises circle the islands but only land in summer.

2 Beara Peninsula
MAP R1 ■ Co Cork and Co Kerry

With its pretty villages, beaches, mountains and walking trails, the Beara Peninsula has something for everyone. The two ranges here are the Slieve Miskish and Caha Mountains. Tortuous bends wend their way to the summits, but it's worth it for the view on fine days. If you are interested in wildlife, it's well worth taking the cable car across to Dursey Island, which is packed with seabird colonies.

3 Killarney
MAP Q2 ■ Co Kerry

On the doorstep of the Ring of Kerry is a wealth of excellent hotels, great pubs with traditional Irish music, as well as old-fashioned ponies and traps, it is not surprising that this attractive town becomes inundated with visitors in summer. The numerous gift shops and restaurants are worth the visit, but the real draw is the beautiful scenery of lakes, mountains and woodland.

4 Dingle
MAP Q1 ■ Co Kerry

A small, attractive fishing town with a fine natural harbour, Dingle is extremely popular with tourists who appreciate its charm. It's a great spot for traditional music, with sessions taking place most evenings in the cosy pubs.

Aerial view of the Bantry House

5 Bantry Bay and Bantry House
MAP R2 ■ Bantry, Co Cork
■ Bantry House: open Apr–Oct: 10am–5pm Tue–Sun; adm; www.bantryhouse.com

This market town and fishing port is named after its beautiful location at the head of Bantry Bay. Bantry House, owned by the White family since 1765, commands outstanding views across the bay and has stunning gardens and a lovely tearoom.

6 **Sneem**
MAP Q1
■ Co Kerry

Popular and charming, backed by the 684-m (2,244-ft) Knockmoyle Mountain, this village resembles something out of a children's picture book, with its houses all painted in bright colours.

7 **Gallarus Oratory**
MAP Q1 ■ Ballydavid, Co Kerry ■ Visitor centre: 066 915 5333

The serenely beautiful Upper Lake, Killarney

The best preserved early Christian site in Ireland is believed to have been built some time between the 7th and 8th centuries. Local legend has it that if you climbed out of the oratory window your soul would be cleansed – an impossible task, since the window is about 18 cm (7 in) long and 12 cm (5 in) wide.

The simple stone Gallarus Oratory

THE SKELLIGS

The history of the Skellig Islands dates back to the 6th century when St Fionán founded the monastery of Skellig Michael. All that remains now are the ruins of the church, two oratories and six beehive cells perched on a narrow platform. From 1821 to 1981, the lighthouses here were looked after by solitary lighthouse keepers. Skellig Michael was designated as a UNESCO World Heritage Site in 1996.

8 **Lakes of Killarney**
MAP Q2 ■ Killarney, Co Kerry

The three lakes in this region, Upper, Middle (Muckross) and Lower (Lough Leane), are linked by the Long Range channel and are all incorporated into the stunning 103-sq-km (40-sq-mile) Killarney National Park. Flanked by mountains, and with a varied landscape of woodland, heather and peat bogs, the area offers a range of beautiful walks and drives.

9 **Kenmare**
MAP Q2 ■ Co Kerry

This prosperous town, designed by the Marquis of Lansdowne in 1775, has more of a continental atmosphere than an Irish one, with its smart shops and fine restaurants. The town is renowned for its traditional lace. During the Famine years (see p39), local nuns introduced lacemaking to create work for the women and girls.

10 **Derrynane House**
MAP Q1 ■ Co Kerry ■ 066 947 5113 ■ Adm

Derrynane is a lovely spot on the coast with 3 km (2 miles) of dunes and beaches. Derrynane House is 2.6 km (1.6 miles) from Caherdaniel and is set in a beautiful parkland. It was the family home of the Catholic politician and lawyer, Daniel O'Connell (see p39). It has been sensitively restored and now contains an interesting museum dedicated to the Great Emancipator.

Places to Eat

 Tom Crean Restaurant
MAP Q2 ▪ Kilowen Rd,
Kenmare ▪ 064 664 1589 ▪ Closed
Mon & Tue ▪ €€

Run by the granddaughter of Arctic
explorer Tom Crean, this restaurant
serves seafood and beer from its
own brewery.

 The Sheen Falls
MAP Q2 ▪ Kenmare, Co Kerry
▪ 064 664 1600 ▪ Closed Jan ▪ €€€

Everything about Sheen Falls lodge
is grand. The Falls restaurant and
the food are equally good.

 QC's Bar & Seafood Restaurant
MAP Q1 ▪ 3 Main St, Cahersiveen
▪ 066 947 2244 ▪ €€

This delightful old bar is full of
character. It has a nautical theme
which extends to the menu – there's
plenty of tasty, chargrilled seafood.

 The Chart House Restaurant
MAP Q1 ▪ The Mall, Dingle ▪ 066 915
2255 ▪ Closed L; winter: Mon & Tue
▪ €€

This family-run restaurant has won
many awards for its delicious food. The
dishes combine many flavours, with
both Asian and European influences.

 Fish Box
MAP Q2 ▪ Upper Green,
Dingle, Co Kerry ▪ Closed Tue
▪ www.thefishboxdingle.com ▪ €€

The menu at this family-owned
seafood bar changes daily depending
on the catch of the day hauled in from
its very own fishing boat. Seafood
doesn't get any fresher than this.

6 **Out of the Blue**
MAP Q2 ▪ Waterside, Dingle,
Co Kerry ▪ 066 915 0811 ▪ €€

Exclusively serving quality seafood
straight from the Atlantic Ocean,
this upmarket restaurant offers
creative dishes. Online reserva-
tions recommended.

 Jam
MAP Q2 ▪ Old Market Lane,
Killarney, Co Kerry ▪ 064 663 7716
▪ Closed D; Sun ▪ €

At Jam, delicious lunch dishes such
as soups, salads, sandwiches and
tarts are made with local produce.

8 **The Half Door**
MAP Q1 ▪ John St, Dingle,
Co Kerry ▪ 066 915 1600 ▪ €€

This cottage-kitchen restaurant
is famed for its generous seafood
platters in lemon butter.

9 **Bantry House**
MAP Q2 ▪ Bantry, Co Cork
▪ 027 50047 ▪ Closed D; Nov–mid-
Apr: Mon ▪ €

This fine house (see p91) overlooking
Bantry Bay has an excellent tearoom.

10 **The Lime Tree**
MAP Q2 ▪ Shelbourne St,
Kenmare ▪ 064 664 1255 ▪ Closed
Nov–Dec: Mon–Fri ▪ €€

Widely acclaimed, this place
serves meals prepared using local
produce. Try the mini portion of
shepherd's pie alongside a rack
of local Kerry lamb.

Dining room at The Lime Tree

See map on p90 ←

TOP 10 Around Cork

Cork city and the surrounding area are full of historic, cultural and scenic places to visit. Cork itself is a lovely city, worth one or two days' exploration, including several islands in Cork harbour formed by the two sections of the River Lee. Cobh, situated on what is known as Great Island, came into its own in the 19th century as an important naval base, owing to its huge natural harbour. Between Cork and Youghal, the small town of Midleton has one of the oldest distilleries in Ireland, Jameson, home to the famous Irish whiskey. The equally well known Blarney Castle, with its "magic" stone, is only a short trip to the north of Cork. To the south, Kinsale is a charming fishing village, a good base for exploring the area.

Panoramic view of Cork City, seen from St Patrick's Hill

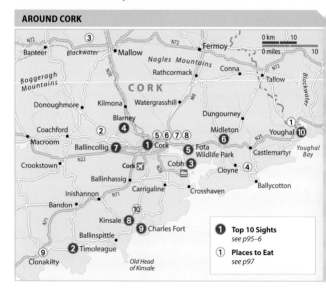

AROUND CORK

❶ **Top 10 Sights**
see p95–6

① **Places to Eat**
see p97

1 Cork City
MAP Q3

Officially Ireland's second city, Cork is a true rival to Dublin according to its 220,000 local residents. Set on an island in the River Lee, the picturesque quays north and south of the river, linked by an array of bridges, offer spectacular views. The waterways, narrow alleys and Georgian buildings, together with the balmy climate, lend the city a more Continental than Irish atmosphere.

2 Timoleague Abbey
MAP R3 ▪ Timoleague

A bleak atmosphere pervades this ruined 13th-century Franciscan abbey, especially when the mist hangs over it. Of particular interest is the wine cellar – the friars imported Spanish wines in the 16th century.

3 Cobh
MAP Q3 ▪ The Queenstown Story: Cobh Heritage Centre; 021 481 3591; open mid-Apr–mid-Oct: 9:30am–6pm (mid-Oct–mid-Apr: until 5pm); adm

Pronounced "Cove", this 19th-century town features one of the world's largest natural harbours. In its heyday, the town was a major commercial seaport as well as being the stopover port for luxury passenger liners, including the *Sirius*, which made her maiden voyage from here. Cobh was also the last port of call for the *Titanic* before she sailed to her tragic end.

Blarney Castle, set in lush gardens

4 Blarney Castle
MAP Q3 ▪ Blarney ▪ 021 438 5252 ▪ Open daily (call ahead for open timings) ▪ Adm

Believed to have been gifted to the King of Munster by Robert the Bruce, the Blarney Stone brings a throng of visitors. Legend has it that whoever kisses the stone will be given the gift of eloquent speech. Now a partial ruin, the castle dates from the mid-15th century, and is surrounded by extensive grounds that feature an ice house, a garden filled with poisonous plants, and a bog garden with waterfalls.

5 Fota Wildlife Park
MAP Q3 ▪ Carrigtohill, Cobh ▪ 021 481 2678 ▪ Open 9:30am–6pm (last adm 4:30pm) ▪ Adm

This large centre, located on Fota Island, is dedicated to conserving animal life as well as reintroducing wild animals to their natural habitats. It also has a highly successful cheetah-breeding programme.

Fishing boats in Cobh harbour

6 Old Midleton Distillery
**MAP Q3 ■ Midleton ■ 021
461 3594 ■ Open daily ■ Adm**

Learn the story of Jameson Irish
Whiskey via an excellent audiovisual
presentation, a tasting and a tour of
the still houses, a distiller's cottage
and the mills and maltings.

Old Midleton Distillery

7 Royal Gunpowder Mills
MAP Q3 ■ Ballincollig

Gunpowder was one of Cork's most
important industries in the mid-19th
century until the mills closed in 1903.
Visitors can see the canals, sluices,
mills and workers' cottages.

8 Kinsale
MAP Q3

The fact that Kinsale has its own
gourmet food festival gives some idea
of the calibre of restaurants and cafés
here. It is probably the most prosperous and sophisticated
fishing village in the
country. Located only
27 km (17 miles) from
Cork city, it attracts

> **CULTURAL CORK**
>
> Cork prides itself on its culture and is
> extremely proud of the Opera House,
> which offers a full programme of
> classical concerts, opera and ballet
> throughout the year. The Triskel Arts
> Centre is the venue for literary events,
> performance art and music. The high-
> profile annual jazz festival in October
> enjoys international status.

locals and tourists in droves. The
pretty harbour is the focal point and
most of the activities centre on this
area and the nearby backstreets.

9 Charles Fort
**MAP Q3 ■ Summer Cove,
Kinsale ■ 021 477 2263 ■ Open
Nov–mid-Mar: 10am–5pm daily; mid-
Mar–Oct: 10am–6pm daily ■ Adm**

Built in the late 17th century, Charles
Fort has been associated with some
of the key events in Irish history,
including the Williamite War (1689–
91) and the Irish Civil War (1922–23).

10 Youghal
MAP Q4

About 50 km (31 miles) east of
Cork city, Youghal (pronounced
"yawl") has a great location on both
the Atlantic Ocean and the River
Blackwater's estuary. The walls
enclosing the town were built by the
English to protect the village from
attack by the native Irish. Queen
Elizabeth I bestowed Youghal on
Sir Walter Raleigh. Under Cromwell,
however, the town became an
English Protestant garrison.

Picturesque street of Kinsale

Places to Eat

1 Aherne's Seafood Restaurant and Bar
MAP Q4 ■ 163 N Main St, Youghal ■ 024 92424 ■ Closed L ■ €€

This is a very popular, elegant restaurant, serving delicious and fresh seafood dishes. It's slightly cheaper to eat in the bar.

2 Blair's Inn
MAP Q3 ■ Cloghroe, Blarney, Co Cork ■ 021 438 1470 ■ €€

An award-winning bar-restaurant, Blair's Inn is full of nooks and crannies, with open fires in winter and a beer garden in summer. Try the excellent fisherman's pie.

3 Longueville House
MAP Q3 ■ Mallow, Co Cork ■ 022 47156 ■ Closed Sun D; Mon–Sat L (winter: Mon–Wed) ■ €€

Set in an elegant country-house, this grand restaurant offers an unforgettable dining experience. The owners brew their own apple brandy, garden berry liqueurs and cider. Coffee is served with handmade chocolates.

4 Ballymaloe House
MAP Q4 ■ Shanagarry ■ 021 465 2531 ■ €€

Darina and Tim Allen's cookery school has a worldwide reputation and it is hardly surprising that the food is absolutely delicious.

5 Elbow Lane Brew and Smokehouse
MAP Q3 ■ 4 Oliver Plunkett St, Cork ■ 021 239 0479 ■ Closed L ■ €€

Set in a handsome townhouse, this "nanobrewery" specializes in delectable dishes from its own smokehouse, alongside tasting trays of its homemade ales.

6 Cask
MAP Q3 ■ 48 MacCurtain St ■ 021 450 0913 ■ Closed Mon–Thu L; Sun ■ €€

Try the tapas-sized street food and tasty cocktails from across the world.

PRICE CATEGORIES
For a three-course meal for one with half a bottle of wine (or equivalent meal), taxes and extra charges.

€ under €45   €€ €45–€90   €€€ over €90

---

7 Café Paradiso
MAP Q3 ■ 16 Lancaster Quay, Cork ■ 021 427 7939 ■ Closed L; Sun ■ €€

This delightful restaurant, with great staff, serves inventive vegetarian cuisine made from quality ingredients.

Relaxed interior of Café Paradiso

8 Greenes
MAP Q3 ■ 48 MacCurtain St, Cork ■ 021 455 2279 ■ Closed Sun–Mon L ■ €€

The windows of this restaurant, set in a converted warehouse, look out onto a 18-m- (60-ft-) high cascade. The food doesn't disappoint, either.

9 An Súgán
MAP R3 ■ 41 Wolf Tone St, Clonakilty ■ 023 883 3719 ■ €€

The West Cork creamy seafood chowder is a hit at this extremely popular restaurant and seafood bar.

10 Fishy Fishy
MAP Q3 ■ Crowley's Quay, Kinsale ■ 021 470 0415 ■ €€

It's no surprise that fresh seafood is always on the menu at the bustling restaurant beside Kinsale's pretty harbour.

See map on p94

🔟 Tipperary, Limerick and Clare

From the lush greenery of Tipperary to the markets of Limerick, and from the pleasure boats cruising on the River Shannon to the stark emptiness of The Burren, this region embraces the full diversity of rural Ireland. There are scores of historic sights and picture-perfect villages, as well as unpretentious country towns with barely any tourist in sight. Cross the Shannon to reach the rockier majesty of County Clare, whose rural way of life retains a profound simplicity. Culturally, it is rooted in tradition, and you'll hear plenty of Irish music played in village pubs. Clare's coastline rises in dramatic cliffs that take the force of the Atlantic, while inland, wind-battered gorse and bracken are broken up by high pasture.

The dramatic cliffs of Moher

1 Cliffs of Moher

MAP N2 ■ Visitors' Centre, Liscannor, Co Clare; 065 708 6141; open Apr–Sep: 8am daily, Oct–Mar: 9am daily; adm

With 14 km (8.6 miles) of dramatic cliffs rising up to 214 m (702 ft) from the Atlantic, this is one of Europe's grandest stretches of coastline. Take the steep cliff-edge footpath round to O'Brien's Tower for some breathtaking views across the ocean.

TIPPERARY, LIMERICK AND CLARE

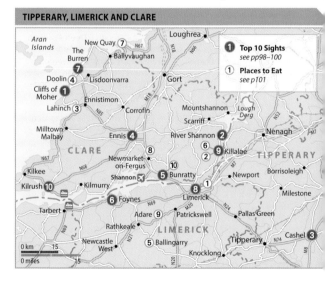

Top 10 Sights
see pp98–100
Places to Eat
see p101

Boats docked at Lough Derg

 River Shannon
MAP P3

Ireland's longest river opens into broad lakes, eventually widening into a huge estuary. The river's curve traditionally marks the border of the west. Lough Derg, the largest lake, is popular for boating and angling.

3 Cashel
MAP N2 ▪ Cashel

This country town is dominated by the Rock of Cashel, topped by stone structures known in pre-Christian times as Cashel of Kings (from Gaelic *caiseal*, a stone fortress). Sensing the rising power of the church, in 1101 the Kings of Munster redefined themselves as a dynasty of royal archbishops and built great ecclesiastical buildings. Most were destroyed by the English in 1647, but highlights of what survives are the 12th-century Cormac's Chapel,

Ireland's earliest Romanesque church; the roofless 13th-century cathedral; and the 15th-century Vicars' Choral, the residential quarters of the cathedral cantors.

4 Ennis
MAP P3 ▪ Friary: 065 682 9100; open Apr–Sep: 10am–6pm; Oct: 10am–5pm; adm

This likeable little town, with its bright shopfronts and music pubs, grew up in the 13th century around Ennis Friary. Shut down in 1692, the abbey fell into ruin but what survives – mostly 15th-century structures – includes the richly carved MacMahon Tomb.

5 Bunratty Castle
MAP P3 ▪ Bunratty ▪ 061 711222 ▪ Open 9:30am–4pm daily ▪ Adm

The sturdy 15th-century stronghold of the O'Briens, Earls of Thomond, has become a top venue for mock medieval banquets and other forms of entertainment. The five-storey structure was fully restored by Viscount Gort in 1954. Behind the castle, Bunratty Folk Park gives an insight into traditional rural culture.

6 Foynes Flying Boat Museum
MAP P2 ▪ Foynes ▪ Open Apr–Oct: 10am–4pm Tue–Sun ▪ Adm

Transatlantic flights between Ireland and the US began in Foynes in 1939, and in 1942 the first non-stop passenger flights between Europe and America started here. The Foynes Flying Boat Museum tells the story through exhibits.

The impressive Rock of Cashel, with its ruined medieval buildings

King John's Castle and Hunt Museum, Limerick

7 The Burren

MAP N2 ■ Burren Centre: Kilfenora; 065 708 8030; open mid-Mar–May, Sep & Oct: 10am–5pm daily; Jun–Aug: 9:30am–5:30pm daily; adm

A weird limestone desert of flat rock "pavements", the 260-sq-km (100-sq-mile) Burren seems mostly lifeless at first glance. But the web of hidden gulleys is brimming with plants, some very rare. Once densely populated, the Burren preserves dolmens, ruined towers and ring-forts. Visit the Burren Centre to learn more.

An ancient dolmen in the Burren

BURREN BOTANY

Apart from seasonal pools, called *turloughs*, the Burren's limestone does not hold water. Yet more than 1,100 plant species thrive here, because countless cracks in the rocks and stones accumulate organic matter and provide shelter. Especially common are mosses, lichens, rock rose, mountain avens, orchids and bloody cranesbill.

8 Limerick

MAP P3 ■ King John's Castle: open 9:30am–5pm daily; adm ■ Hunt Museum: Rutland St; open 10am–5pm Mon–Sat, 2–5pm Sun; adm

A grim portrait of industrial Limerick, the third-largest city in the republic, was painted by Frank McCourt's novel *Angela's Ashes* (see p43). However, it has improved significantly now. The city centre has great restaurants and pubs and a pleasant atmosphere. Historical sights include the imposing King John's Castle, built in 1210. The Hunt Museum, with its collection of Irish antiquities, is also worth a visit.

9 Killaloe

MAP P3

A chic marina town rising steeply from the southern end of Lough Derg, Killaloe is a centre for watersports. The 12th-century St Flannan's Cathedral and Oratory have fine Romanesque decorative stonework.

10 Kilrush and Loop Head Drive

MAP P2 ■ Museum of Rural Life: open 9am–6pm Mon–Sat; adm

This 18th-century estate town makes a good base for exploring the furthest reaches of southwest County Clare. A drive out to Loop Head provides superb views. For an insight into local history, visit the fascinating Museum of Rural Life, which features artifacts from World War II and John F Kennedy's historic trip to Ireland.

See map on p98

Places to Eat

 Copper and Spice
MAP P3 ■ Annacotty Village, Limerick ■ 061 338791 ■ Closed Tue ■ €

A stylish restaurant that presents Indian-Asian cuisine, with lots of good options for vegetarians. There is a take-away menu too.

 Flanagan's on the Lake
MAP P3 ■ Ballina Killaloe ■ 061 622 790 ■ €

While tucking into spicy wings, ribs and burgers, enjoy the view of passing boats from Flanagan's. It offers an excellent selection of whiskeys, too.

 Barrtrá Seafood Restaurant
MAP N2 ■ Miltown Malbay Rd, Lahinch, Co Clare ■ 065 708 1280 ■ www.barrtra.com ■ €€

This homely cliff-side, bay-facing cottage is an institution. Barrtrá serves wonderful steaks and seafood.

 Cullinans
MAP N2 ■ Doolin ■ 065 707 4183 ■ Closed L; Sun; mid-Oct–Easter ■ €€

A family-owned restaurant (and guesthouse) in the centre of Doolin village, Cullinans is renowned for its locally caught fresh seafood.

5 The Mustard Seed
MAP P3 ■ Echo Lodge, Ballingarry ■ 069 68508 ■ www.mustardseed.ie ■ €€

Set within a Victorian country-house hotel, this stylish restaurant offers award-winning modern Irish cuisine as well as an excellent wine list.

PRICE CATEGORIES
For a three-course meal for one with half a bottle of wine (or equivalent meal), taxes and extra charges.

€ under €45　€€ €45–€90　€€€ over €90

6 The Wooden Spoon
MAP P3 ■ Bridge St, Killaloe ■ 061 622 415 ■ €

This welcoming and friendly café that serves delicious sweet and savoury treats is ideal for lunch.

7 Linnane's Lobster Bar
MAP N2 ■ The Pier, New Quay ■ 065 707 8120 ■ Closed Nov–mid-Mar: Mon–Thu ■ €

Stunning views of the Burren and Aughinish Island complement the delicious seafood on offer here.

8 Earl of Thomond
MAP P3 ■ Newmarket-on-Fergus ■ 061 368144 ■ €€€

Dromoland Castle is the perfect place for a grand meal after a day on the adjoining golf course.

9 1826 Adare
MAP P3 ■ Blackabbey, Adare ■ 061 396 004 ■ Closed Mon–Wed ■ €€

Seasonal cuisine prepared from local produce is served in an intimate setting in one Ireland's prettiest villages.

10 Durty Nelly's Oyster Restaurant
MAP P3 ■ Bunratty ■ 061 364861 ■ €€

Set in the shadow of Bunratty Castle, this thatched inn, in business since 1620, serves oysters and steaks.

Durty Nelly's Oyster Restaurant

TOP10 Clonmacnoise and the Midlands

1 Belvedere House

MAP N4 ▪ N52, Mullingar ▪ 044 933 8960 ▪ Open hours vary, call ahead to check ▪ Adm

There was no sense or sensibility in the actions of the Earl of Belvedere, despite the Austen-style setting of his house. He began the house in 1740, spent his life fighting his brothers and built the Gothic Jealous Wall to block the view of his sibling's house. He also locked up his wife for 31 years, suspecting she'd slept with one of them.

Elegant interiors at Belvedere House

2 Tullynally Castle

MAP M4 ▪ Castlepollard ▪ 044 966 1856 ▪ Castle: tours daily (closed Sun); Gardens: open Apr–Oct: 11am–5pm Thu–Sun; adm

Constructed in the 17th century, most of Tullynally today is a result of the second Earl of Longford's remodelling of it as a Gothic Revival castle, housing a collection of Irish furniture and portraits. Outside are romantic grounds.

3 Emo Court

MAP N4 ▪ Portlaoise ▪ 057 862 6573 ▪ House: open Easter–Sep: 10am–6pm daily; Gardens: open dawn–dusk daily; adm (to house)

Designed in 1790 for the Earl of Portarlington,

this is another fine example of architect James Gandon's work, and his interiors in this lovely house remain unchanged. The gardens are divided into two sections: the Grapery leads you down to a lakeside walk; the Clucker acquired its name from the nuns who used to reside here.

4 Kilbeggan Distillery

MAP N4 ▪ Kilbeggan, Co Westmeath ▪ 057 933 2134 ▪ Open 10am–5:30pm daily (last adm 1 hr before closing) ▪ Adm ▪ www.kilbeggandistillery.com

Originally known as Locke's, the distillery closed in 1953, two centuries after getting its licence in 1757. In the years that followed, the building was restored and run as a whiskey museum. In 2010, a new distillery was added and is open for tours and tastings.

5 Clonmacnoise

MAP N4 ▪ Shannonbridge ▪ 0909 674195 ▪ Open Feb–mid-Mar: 10am–5:30pm daily (last adm 4:45pm); mid-Mar–Oct: 10am–5:30pm daily (last adm 5pm); Nov–Jan: 10am–5pm daily (last adm 4pm) ▪ Adm

This early Christian site, founded by St Ciaran in the 6th century, draws tourists into Ireland's often neglected Midlands. The grounds are atmospheric, especially on a grey Irish day, and include the ruins of a cathedral, seven churches (10th–13th centuries), two round towers, three high crosses and dozens of early Christian grave slabs. The visitors' centre offers an audiovisual history of the site and various exhibitions.

Celtic Cross at Clonmacnoise

Impressive Birr Castle, dating back to medieval times

6 Birr Castle, Gardens and Science Centre

MAP N4 ▪ Birr ▪ 057 912 0336 ▪ Open mid-Mar–Oct: 9am–6pm daily; Nov–mid-Mar: 10am–4:30pm daily ▪ Adm

The award-winning gardens are the highlight here, with 2,000 species of rare trees, shrubs and flowers and wonderful wildlife, as well as a lake and waterfalls. Birr's grounds also host a Science Centre, featuring the third Earl of Rosse's 1840s telescope, which for decades was the largest in the world. The earl's discovery of spiralling galaxies is brought to life by the centre's interactive exhibits.

7 Birr
MAP N4

Although dominated by the castle and its grounds, the town of Birr has much to offer visitors. Its beautiful Georgian buildings have been preserved, with many houses retaining their original fanlights and door panelling.

8 Slieve Bloom Mountains
MAP N4

Despite only rising 527 m (1,729 ft), the surrounding flat plain aids in creating an imposing image of the Slieve Bloom Mountains, a National Nature Reserve. The 75-km- (47-mile-) Slieve Bloom Way has been marked out for hikers.

9 Bog of Allen
MAP N5 ▪ Bog of Allen Nature Centre, Lullymore: 045 860133; open 9am–5pm Mon–Fri

Once the largest raised peat bog in Ireland, the Bog of Allen has been gradually shrinking after many centuries of agricultural exploitation. It is home to some of Ireland's most interesting indigenous plants and insects, including the carnivorous sundew and Venus Fly Trap.

10 Rock of Dunamase
MAP N4 ▪ Laois

Towering 45 m (150 ft) above a flat plain, the Rock of Dunamase, with its castle ruins, is one of the most impressive and historic sights in Ireland. The sight was included on Ptolemy's world map in 140 CE, such was its fame, and the ruins date back thousands of years. Standing here, you can see all the way to the Slieve Bloom Mountains.

The ruins of Dunamase Castle

🔟 Around Galway

County Galway has a peculiar majesty and a sense of its closeness to nature, stalwartly facing the Atlantic Ocean. Even the area around the county town, Galway City, squeezed onto a strip of land between the expanse of Lough Corrib and the immense waters of Galway Bay, possesses that same inspiring quality. With its fine restaurants and charming pubs, Galway is a good base from which to explore the area. South of the city is a gentler, greener countryside. While a good deal of the fascination of this southern edge of Galway lies simply in the landscape, for lovers of literature much of the interest is also in the connection with the romantic Irish poet W B Yeats. Although not originally from this region, Yeats spent many years living at Thoor Ballylee near Gort.

The Claddagh, an old fishing village near Galway city centre

AROUND GALWAY

- **1** Top 10 Sights
  see pp105–6
- ① Places to Eat
  see p107

Kilmaine · Clonbur ⑦ · ④ Cong · Belclare · ① Tuam
Lough Corrib ⑥ · Headford
Cashel · Oughterard ②
Gortmore · Rosscahill · Cloonboo
Kilkieran · GALWAY · Moycullen ⑤ · Claregalway
Casla · ③ ④ ⑨ · Athenry
Rossaveel · Galway ① · ⑤
Inveran · R336 · Galway · ⑥ Oranmore
Spiddal ③ · Barna · ② Clarinbridge
Galway Bay · Kilcolgan
⑧ Kilronan · ⑩ · Ardrahan
Aran Islands · Kinvara ⑨
Ballyvaughan · Coole Park ⑩ · ⑦ Thoor Ballylee
Burren · Kilmacduagh ⑧ · Gort
Doolin · Lisdoonvarna · Monastery
Kilfenora

0 km 10
0 miles 10

1 Galway City
MAP N3

This pleasant, bustling regional capital started life as a fortress of the O'Connors of Connacht. Colonized in 1235 by Anglo-Normans, it became a prosperous seaport. Some fine buildings survive, notably 16th-century Lynch's Castle (now a bank), and 14th-century St Nicholas's Church. There's a great atmosphere, with plenty of music and traditional shops.

The crumbling ruins of Athenry Dominican Priory

2 Oughterard
MAP N2 ■ Aughnanure Castle: open Mar–Oct: 9:30am–6pm daily; Nov: 9:30am–4pm daily; adm

Located on the shores of Lough Corrib, this village has become a small resort area. Aughnanure Castle, a highlight, is set beside the lake. It is a handsome remnant of a 16th-century tower house of the O'Flaherty clan of Connacht, who terrorized the ruling Anglo-Norman families of Galway.

3 Spiddal
MAP N2

Officially Irish-speaking, and hosting a Gaelic summer school, Spiddal makes a pleasant stop on the Galway Bay coast road. In the Spiddal Craft Village, you can see several crafts such as pottery, weaving, and other skilled work in progress, as well as buy the beautiful finished goods.

4 Cong Abbey
MAP M2 ■ Cong

Poised on the narrow strip between Lough Corrib and Lough Mask, the attractive village of Cong lies just across the Galway border in County Mayo. Cong Abbey was an important Augustinian community founded by the King of Connacht in 1120. Closed down during the Reformation, it fell into ruin. What survives, including the lovely cloisters, remains majestic.

5 Athenry
MAP N3

The poignant folksong "The Fields of Athenry" (pronounced "athen-rye") gives little clue about this evocative reminder of the Anglo-Norman colonists. In 1235, Meyler de Bermingham was granted a charter to Athenry, where he built a little castle and founded a Dominican Priory in 1241 where he and his descendants could be buried. Today, though damaged, much survives, together with a broken 15th-century cross erected in the central square.

6 Lough Corrib
MAP N2

The vast expanse of Lough Corrib's cool waters, feeling more like part of the Atlantic Ocean, is Ireland's second largest lake, and a popular resort area for angling, various watersports and walking.

Serene and idyllic Lough Corrib

TO BE CARVED

One of W B Yeats's poems is entitled *To Be Carved on a Stone at Thoor Ballylee*, and the words have indeed been carved at Yeats's old tower house: "I, the poet William Yeats, / With old mill boards and sea-green slates, / And smithy work from the Gort forge, / Restored this tower for my wife George; / And may these characteristics remain / When all is ruin once again."

7 Thoor Ballylee
MAP N3 ■ Gort ■ 091 537 700
■ Open Apr: 11am–4pm Sat & Sun;
May: 11am–4pm daily (Jun–Sep:
until 5pm) ■ Adm ■ www.yeatsthoor
ballylee.org

The old tower house in which W B Yeats and his wife Georgie spent much time during the 1920s is a sturdy little fortress. Restored and converted by Yeats, it is described with touching detail in many of his poems.

8 Kilmacduagh Monastery
MAP N3 ■ Gort

An astonishing set of monastic abbey ruins survive here. The original church, established in 610, was enlarged over the centuries and replaced by a cathedral in the 11th or 12th century, though keeping many features of the older buildings, including an 11th-century door. Around it are other intriguing 13th- and 14th-century buildings. There's even a "Leaning Tower", built in the 10th century.

Cows grazing the grounds of Kilmacduagh Monastery

Boats at Kinvara's fishing harbour

9 Kinvara
MAP N3

The little road around Galway Bay passes through a score of villages that are breathtaking in their prettiness and grandiose location. The most charming is Kinvara, with its fishing harbour and pier cottages. It's the setting for a traditional music festival in May, and a Gathering of the Boats festival in August.

10 Coole Park
MAP N3 ■ Gort ■ Open summer: 8am–7:30pm daily; winter: 8am–6pm daily
■ www.coolepark.ie

The woods, lakes and paths of this national park and wildlife reserve, with its red deer, were once the grounds of a great Georgian mansion, home of Lady Augusta Gregory. Augusta hosted the most famous novelists and playwrights of her day and the Irish Revival began here.

Places to Eat

(1) Cre na Cille
MAP M3 ▪ High St, Tuam ▪ 093
28232 ▪ Closed L; Sun & Mon ▪ €€

Seafood, steaks and game are the specialities of this excellent, unassuming family-run restaurant. It also has an array of fine whiskeys.

(2) Paddy Burke's Oyster Inn
MAP N3 ▪ Clarinbridge ▪ 091 796
226 ▪ €€

A good time to visit this pub is during Clarinbridge's oyster festival in September. It offers a choice of good meat and fish dishes, as well as shellfish from the famed local beds.

Fun interior of Ard Bia at Nimmos

(3) Ard Bia at Nimmos
MAP N3 ▪ Spanish Arch, Galway City ▪ 091 561 114 ▪ €€

Restaurant, café, art gallery – the reputable Ard Bia at Nimmos, offers an Irish menu with global influences spanning breakfast, brunch, lunch, tea and dinner.

(4) The Seafood Bar @ Kirwan's Lane
MAP N3 ▪ Kirwan's Lane, Galway City ▪ 091 568 266 ▪ Closed Sun L ▪ €€

This brasserie-style restaurant, with a lively atmosphere, serves creative seafood dishes with a flair. The daily specials are highly recommended.

PRICE CATEGORIES
For a three-course meal for one with half a bottle of wine (or equivalent meal), taxes and extra charges.
....
€ under €45　€€ €45–€90　€€€ over €90

---

(5) White Gables
MAP N2 ▪ Moycullen Village
▪ 091 555 744 ▪ Closed L; Mon–Wed; 25 Dec–mid-Feb ▪ €€

Set in a 19th-century inn, White Gables is best known for its time warp classics such as seafood cocktail and halibut Veronique.

(6) Pins Gastro Bar
MAP N2 ▪ The Twelve Hotel, Barna Village, Galway ▪ 091 597 000 ▪ €

The emphasis is on top-quality locally sourced produce at this restaurant. It serves pizzas and modern Irish food.

(7) Burke's Bar and Restaurant
MAP N3 ▪ Mount Gable House, Clonbur, Co Galway ▪ 094 954 6175
▪ Restaurant: Closed L ▪ €€

Expect a warm welcome, hearty cuisine, live traditional music and great craic at this classic Irish pub.

(8) Teach Nan Phaidi
MAP P2 ▪ Kilmurvey, Inis Mór
▪ 099 20975 ▪ Closed 20–25 Dec ▪ €

Set in a thatched cottage, this cosy café serves good food. Do not miss the Guinness chocolate cake.

(9) McDonagh's
MAP N3 ▪ 22 Quay St, Galway City ▪ 091 565 001 ▪ Closed L; Sun ▪ €

Since generations, this restaurant is known as one of the country's finest fish-and-chip shops.

(10) The Pier Head
MAP N3 ▪ The Quay, Kinvara
▪ 091 638 188 ▪ €€

Overlooking the bay, this place serves hearty portions of Irish and European fare. Try the Atlantic Seafood chowder.

See map on p104 ◁

🔟 Connemara and Mayo

Connemara – the rocky, mountainous countryside of western County Galway – is largely uncultivated, and is a strange wilderness of water and stone, peat bog, headlands and barren hills. Along its shores, the Atlantic eats into the land, making spectacular inlets and bays. Thousands of rough dry-stone walls criss-cross the bare hills, enclosing tiny abandoned fields. The famine wiped out most of Connemara's population, and the memory of that disaster lingers in the glorious landscape. Across Killary Fjord and into County Mayo, you'll find appealing small towns and a traditional way of life, as well as wide open spaces of bog, heath, mountain and lake.

The Sky Road with its scenic views

① Sky Road
MAP M1

Named for its beautiful cliff-edge ocean views, the Sky Road is a 16-km (10-mile) loop that starts out from Clifden, and skirts the narrow peninsula alongside Clifden Bay. Along the way you'll see empty beaches, fabulous wild hill scenery, and sights such as the ruins of Neo-Gothic Clifden Castle, the home of Clifden's founder John d'Arcy.

CONNEMARA AND MAYO

Picturesque Roundstone harbour, with its lobster-fishing boats

② Roundstone
MAP N2

Officially known as Cloch na Rón, this Irish-speaking, attractively laid out and "planned village" was built in the 1820s. This unassuming lobster-fishing community also has an arty side and is packed with multiple attractions which include a good beach, galleries and traditional shops.

③ Westport
MAP M2 ▪ Westport House: open hours vary, check website; adm; www.westporthouse.ie

Busy and popular, Westport is a small enough country town that can easily be seen from the end of the main streets. Laid out with wide tree-lined streets and dignified central Octagon, Westport is a good example of a planned town. It was built in 1780 by the Earl of Altamont as an adjunct to his mansion, the Westport House. The limestone mansion remains imposing and grandly furnished, with a number of attractions such as a pirate adventure park for children.

④ Connemara National Park and Twelve Bens Mountains
MAP M2 ▪ Visitors' Centre: Letterfrack; 095 41054; open 9am–5:30pm daily

Extending from Letterfrack village to the Twelve Bens, the Connemara National Park is a lovely 20-sq-km (8-sq-mile) conservation area of heath, bog and hills that make up the grandest of Connemara's landscapes. The Twelve Bens, comprises of a dozen high peaks that rise from the heart of the western mountains, dominating Connemara's skyline. The visitor centre near the park entrance has a permanent exhibition on the flora, fauna, geology and history of the region.

Sheep in Connemara National Park

⑤ Clifden
MAP M1

Framed by the lovely green hills above Clifden Bay and grandeur of the Twelve Bens Mountains, this early 19th-century market town passes for the "capital" of Connemara region. This Georgian planned town, built by John d'Arcy, retains a certain character and style. At the end of summer, Clifden hosts the Connemara Pony Show, which attracts horse-lovers.

The beautifully sited Kylemore Abbey, next to Kylemore Lough

6 Kylemore Abbey

MAP M2 ■ Kylemore ■ 095 52001 ■ Open Apr–Oct: 10am–6pm daily (last adm 5pm) ■ Adm

The extraordinarily elaborate mock-Gothic castle, built in 1868 for millionaire Mitchell Henry, has been a Benedictine convent since the 1920s. Although a religious community, it is also run as a commercial tourist attraction. The house and walled gardens are magnificently located, next to Kylemore Lough, with views towards the Twelve Bens.

7 Clare and Inishbofin Islands

MAP M1

Dramatic Clare Island was the stronghold of Grace O'Malley, or Granuaile, whose little fortress still stands, as does the ruined abbey where she was buried. Inishbofin has a green, lonely beauty. Home of the O'Flaherty clan and a hideaway of Grace O'Malley, it was taken over by Cromwell. Both islands have small populations and prehistoric ruins.

8 Leenane to Killary Harbour

MAP M2

The appealing village of Leenane lies beside the long, narrow inlet of Killary Fjord. From here, the dramatically beautiful road to the small oceanside resort of Louisburgh crosses the water between the peaks of Devil's Mother and Ben Gorm, and rises among lakes and streams along the narrow Delphi Valley.

9 Céide Fields

MAP L2 ■ Open Apr, May & Oct: 10am–5pm daily (Jun–Sep: until 6pm) ■ Adm

Preserved for thousands of years under a blanket of peat bog, the Céide site consists of walled fileds from the Stone Age, along with other stone ruins. Excellent guided tours are offered by the visitor centre.

10 Croagh Patrick

MAP M2

This is one of the most sacred sites in Ireland. St Patrick fasted on the summit for 40 days in 441 CE. It is considered a pious act to make the steep climb up to the summit.

Pilgrims ascending Croagh Patrick

GRACE O'MALLEY

Grace O'Malley (1530–1603) was the daughter of a Connacht chieftain. At 15, she married the O'Flaherty chief, whose men remained loyal to her after his death. With fortresses throughout Connacht, and based on Clare Island, she visited Queen Elizabeth I in 1593, extracting a promise to be left in peace.

Places to Eat

PRICE CATEGORIES

For a three-course meal for one with half a bottle of wine (or equivalent meal), taxes and extra charges.

€ under €45 €€ €45–€90 €€€ over €90

1 O'Dowd's Seafood Bar and Restaurant

MAP N2 ▪ Roundstone ▪ 095 35809 ▪ €

Fresh Connemara mussels, beef and Guinness pie are served here. A bowl of O'Dowd's delicious chowder is a joy on a cloudy day.

2 La Fougère

MAP M2 ▪ Knockranny House Hotel, Westport, Co Mayo ▪ 098 28600 ▪ Closed L ▪ €€

This award-winning restaurant is set on a hill and is a short walk from the town centre. It offers delicious fare.

3 Kylemore Kitchen

MAP M2 ▪ Kylemore Abbey, Connemara, Co Galway ▪ 095 52001 ▪ Closed D ▪ €

The Connemara lamb pasty and Irish stew served here are made with produce from the abbey's garden. Try the homemade cakes.

4 Rosleague Manor

MAP M2 ▪ Letterfrack ▪ 095 41101 ▪ Open to non-residents by reservation ▪ €€

Connemara lamb and local seafood are specialities of the house, served with the best local ingredients.

5 Poacher

MAP L2 ▪ Ballina ▪ 096 77982 ▪ €€

This smart bistro serves the best local and foraged food. It's great for vegetarians and vegans, too.

6 Newport House

MAP M2 ▪ Newport ▪ 098 41222 ▪ €€

Set in a lovely Georgian mansion, this restaurant bases its menu on fresh produce from its own farm, gardens and fishery, and smokes its own salmon. What's more, it features a superb wine cellar.

7 Renvyle House

MAP M1 ▪ Renvyle ▪ 095 46100 ▪ €€

A gracious country-house hotel on the shores of the Atlantic serves superb seafood, Connemara lamb and other classic Irish and European dishes. Booking is highly recommended.

8 Mitchell's

MAP M1 ▪ Market St, Clifden, Co Galway ▪ 095 21867 ▪ Closed Nov–Mar ▪ €€

An excellent family-style restaurant, Mitchell's serves comforting, home-style food, such as seafood and poultry dishes, in a relaxed setting.

Stylish interior of JW's Brasserie

9 JW's Brasserie

MAP M2 ▪ The Octagon, Westport, Co Mayo ▪ 098 25027 ▪ €

Housed in the Wyatt Hotel, this award-winning contemporary Irish restaurant is popular with locals and visitors alike.

10 Cashel House

MAP N2 ▪ Cashel ▪ 095 31001 ▪ €€

Previously a gracious aristocratic home, this country house and restaurant has now earned itself international renown for both its food and atmosphere.

See map on p108

🔟 Yeats Country and the Northwest

The Northwest includes some of Ireland's most dramatic scenery, with its beautiful wide sandy beaches, towering mountains, woodland and forest parks. Driving is the best way to tour this part of the country as public transport is all but non-existent. The region's colloquial name is in honour of the two great Irish brothers, Jack B and W B Yeats, artist and poet respectively, who spent much of their boyhood in the ancient Celtic town of Sligo. Also the legendary power base of the warrior Queen Maeve of Connaught, it is packed with prehistoric sites. Donegal was left isolated when it was excluded from the new Northern Ireland in 1921 and has little in common with its fellow counties.

Mount Errigal, Glenveagh National Park

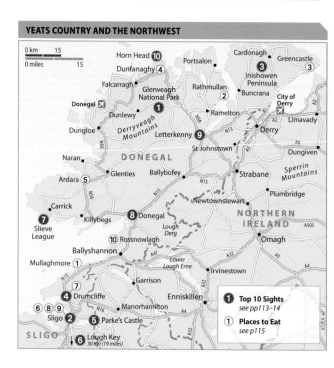

YEATS COUNTRY AND THE NORTHWEST

1 Top 10 Sights
see pp113–14

1 Places to Eat
see p115

1 Glenveagh National Park

MAP K4 ■ Co Donegal ■ 076 100 2537 ■ Park: open dusk to dawn daily; Visitor Centre: open mid-Mar–Oct: 9am–5:30pm daily; Nov–mid-Mar: 9am–5pm daily

The extraordinary quartzite cone of Mount Errigal dominates the Derryveagh mountain range in this wild part of Donegal. It overlooks the Glenveagh National Park, which incorporates the beautiful Lough Veagh Valley, and Poison Glen.

2 Sligo

MAP L3 ■ Co Sligo

This busy market town is home to the Model Arts Centre and Niland Gallery, which has a collection of Jack B Yeats's paintings, as well as quirky, art shops, bookshops and fine restaurants. To the east of town is Lough Gill, which has a number of woodland walks, while Benbulben Mountain and the sandy beaches of Strandhill and Rosses Point are only a 10-minute drive away.

3 Inishowen Peninsula

MAP K4 ■ Co Donegal

Undiscovered by so many, this glorious corner in the far northwest has possibly the finest scenery in Ireland, with the spectacular Slieve Snaght Mountain in the centre, Foyle and Swilly lakes to the east and west, and the dune-fringed beaches facing the Atlantic. The peninsula also has its share of dramatic headlands and features Ireland's most northwesterly point at rugged Malin Head.

Drumcliffe church, built in 1809

4 Lissadell and Drumcliffe

MAP L3 ■ Ballinfull, Co Sligo ■ Lissadell House: open mid-Apr–Oct; www.lissadellhouse.com

North of Sligo is Drumcliffe church, where W B Yeats (see p42) is buried. The visitors' centre focuses on items and books relating to Yeats who was a frequent visitor at nearby Lissadell House, home to the Gore-Booth family, who fought for Irish freedom.

5 Parke's Castle

MAP L3 ■ Fivemilebourne, Co Leitrim ■ 086 071 6968 ■ Open Apr–Sep: 10am–6pm daily ■ Adm

Overlooking Lough Gill, this moated, fortified manor house, accessible by road or boat, was erected on the site of an earlier house. Much of the earlier structure is incorporated into the castle, but otherwise it is a fine example of a Plantation house.

Five-Finger Strand at Malin Head

Castle Island, with its romantic folly castle, on Lough Key

6 Lough Key and Boyle
MAP M3 ■ Co Roscommon

One of the best spots for viewing this magnificent lake is from the main Sligo-to-Boyle road. The Lough Key Forest Park has numerous walks along the lakeside and through the woods. Nearby is the appealing town of Boyle, with a ruined abbey, interesting museum and some very fine Georgian architecture.

7 Slieve League
MAP L3 ■ Co Donegal
■ **Slieve League Cliffs Centre:** www.slieveleaguecliffs.ie

Europe's highest accessible sea cliffs plunge some 600 m (1,970 ft) into the Atlantic – that's almost three times higher than the more famous Cliffs of Moher *(see p98)*. The viewing platform can be reached via a precipitous 6-km (4-mile) drive from Teelin village, passing the Slieve League Cliffs Centre, with its café, craft shop and art gallery, on the way.

8 Donegal
MAP L4 ■ Co Donegal

Donegal is most famous for its tweed production, with Magee of Donegal the biggest manufacturer based here. The Diamond, a triangular central market, is at the heart of the town and an obelisk in the centre commemorates the four Gaelic Franciscans who wrote *The Annals of the Four Masters* in the 1630s. This extraordinary opus follows the history of the Gaelic people from the Great Flood up to the 17th century.

THE GAELTACHTS

The area around Donegal is one of the largest Gaelic-speaking *(Gaeltacht)* regions of the country. Until the 17th century most of the Irish population spoke Gaelic, the only other language being Latin. During British rule, use of the language diminished as English took over, but it is steadily reviving.

9 Letterkenny
MAP K4 ■ Co Donegal

County Donegal's largest town is flanked to the west by the Derryveagh Mountains and the Sperrin Mountains to the east. Visit the Gothic St Eunan's Cathedral and the County Museum.

10 Horn Head
MAP K4 ■ Co Donegal

This dramatic 180-m (600-ft) rock face, with stupendous views over the Atlantic, is home to hundreds of seabirds, including gulls and puffins.

The dramatic cliffs of Horn Head

Places to Eat

1 Eithna's by the Sea
MAP L3 ▪ The Harbour, Mullaghmore, Co Sligo ▪ 071 916 6407 ▪ www.eithnasrestaurant.com ▪ €€

At this bracing, long-established harbourside spot in Mullaghmore, the owner Eithna O'Sullivan does wonders with lobster, hake, clams and mussels – the seaweed pesto is so good that it's sold in jars. Try to get a table outdoors.

2 The Cook & Gardener
MAP K4 ▪ Rathmullan House, Co Donegal ▪ 074 915 8188 ▪ Closed Jan–mid Feb ▪ €€

Gourmet dinners are made with local ingredients, sourced from the walled organic garden, and served in this grand country-house hotel.

Oysters at Kealy's Seafood Bar

3 Kealy's Seafood Bar
MAP K5 ▪ Greencastle, Co Donegal ▪ 074 938 1010 ▪ Closed Mon–Wed ▪ €

This atmospheric restaurant-bar serves great seafood and a range of meat and vegetarian dishes. There's traditional Irish music most Sundays.

4 The Rusty Oven
MAP K4 ▪ Dunfanaghy, Co Donegal ▪ Closed Nov–Feb L ▪ www.therustyoven.ie ▪ €€

Creative, handmade sourdough pizzas are the speciality of this casual outdoor restaurant. The menu also includes a chocolate pizza for dessert.

PRICE CATEGORIES

For a three-course meal for one with half a bottle of wine (or equivalent meal), taxes and extra charges.

€ under €45   €€ €45–€90   €€€ over €90

5 Woodhill House
MAP K3 ▪ Ardara, Co Donegal ▪ 074 954 1112 ▪ €€

This coastal manor house has a superb French-style restaurant. Try the fresh seafood landed at the nearby fishing village of Killybegs.

6 Coach Lane Restaurant
MAP L3 ▪ 1–2 Lord Edward St, Sligo ▪ 071 916 2417 ▪ €€

Sample a delicious variety of cooking styles and dishes, such as Sligo Bay oysters and dry-aged Irish beef as well as local Lissadell mussels and clams.

7 Yeats Tavern
MAP L3 ▪ Drumcliffe, Co Sligo ▪ 071 916 3117 ▪ Closed winter: Fri–Sun ▪ €

A popular stopping place on the way to Donegal, the helpings here are generous and there's a variety of choice.

8 Montmartre
MAP L3 ▪ 1 Market Yard, Sligo, Co Sligo ▪ 071 916 9901 ▪ Closed Mon; Tue–Sat L; Sun D ▪ €€

The creative menus here feature French and European cuisine, and the wine list is excellent.

9 Fiddlers Creek
MAP L3 ▪ Rockwood Parade, Sligo, Co Sligo ▪ 071 914 1866 ▪ €

Enjoy gastro-pub classics such as wings and burgers alongside live music at this bar and restaurant.

10 Smuggler's Creek Inn
MAP L3 ▪ Rossnowlagh, Co Donegal ▪ 071 985 2366 ▪ Closed Oct–late May: Sun–Thu ▪ €€

Take a table with a view in this family-run restaurant overlooking the sweep of Donegal Bay.

See map on p112

🔟 Northern Ireland

Northern Ireland remained under UK administration when the rest of Ireland became independent in 1921. A distinctive society has developed here, rooted in the historic cultural divide between Nationalists (Catholics of Irish descent) and Loyalists (Protestants of English and Scottish descent). Yet between Northern Ireland and the Republic there are more similarities than differences, from music to food and drink. The region has some of the most stunning landscapes in the country.

The extraordinary rock formations at the Giant's Causeway

NORTHERN IRELAND

- ① **Top 10 Sights**
  see pp117–18
- ① **Places to Eat**
  see p119

Giant's Causeway ②
Portrush
Portstewart
⑧ Bushmills Ballycastle
Coleraine Cushendall
Ballymoney
Carnlough
⑨
Limavady Garvagh ⑤ Glens of Antrim
⑩ Derry (Londonderry)
Letterkenny
Ballymena Larne
Strabane
Maghera
Magherafelt Carrickfergus
NORTHERN IRELAND
Antrim Bangor
Belfast ✈
Ulster-American ⑦ Folk Park
Cookstown
Belfast ③
⑤
Pettigoe Omagh ② ③ ⑥ ⑦ ⑩ Mount Stewart House
Dungannon Lough Neagh Lisburn ⑨
Irvinestown
⑥
Lower Lough Erne Portadown Lurgan Portaferry ①
Enniskillen ④ Armagh Downpatrick
⑧ Dundrum ④ Castle Ward
Florence Court Monaghan Newry Newcastle

0 km 20
0 miles 20

1 Castle Ward
MAP L6 ■ Strangford, Co Down
■ 028 448 81204 ■ House: open Mar–
Oct (hours vary, call ahead to check);
Grounds: open all year ■ Adm

Strikingly set beside Strangford
Lough, this 18th-century mansion
has been home to the Ward family
since 1570. There are numerous
walking and cycling trails in the
landscaped grounds. Also sited in
the grounds, the estate's Clearsky
Adventure Centre offers archery
beside the medieval tower house,
which starred as "Winterfell" in
the drama series *Game of Thrones*.

2 Giant's Causeway
MAP K5 ■ Bushmills, Co
Antrim ■ 028 2073 1855

The Giant's Causeway, designated a
World Heritage Site since 1986, is
a truly remarkable natural spectacle,
its thousands of extraordinary hexa-
gonal pillars of basalt rock clustered
like a gigantic piece of honeycomb.
The rocks descend from seafront
cliffs into the water and disappear
from view. Supposedly created
by legendary warrior Fionn mac
Cumhaill *(see p45)* as his stepping
stones to Scotland, the Causeway
was really created by a volcanic
eruption some 60 million years ago.

3 Belfast
MAP L6 ■ Belfast Welcome
Centre: 9 Donegall Sq N; open daily

Northern Ireland's capital is a vibrant
Victorian city with shops, pubs, museums and galleries. Call at the Belfast
Welcome Centre for details of the
city's attractions, such as the absorb-
ing Titanic Belfast museum.

The Titanic Belfast

St Patrick's Cathedral, Armagh

4 Armagh
MAP L5

The city where Queen Macha built
her fortress some 3,000 years ago,
Armagh has a curious role in Ulster's
religious divide. St Patrick based
himself here, and the city is considered the ecclesiastical capital of both
communities, with both a Catholic
and a Protestant cathedral.

5 Glens of Antrim
MAP K5

Among the finest scenery in Ireland
is the coast of County Antrim, where
nine beautiful valleys (glens) cut
deeply through high rolling hills to
descend grandly into the sea. Follow
the A2 through Carnlough, with its
harbour, through Waterfoot, with
waterfalls and a Forest Park, all
the way up to the Giant's Causeway.

6 Lower Lough Erne
MAP L4

The serene waters and small islands
extending north from Enniskillen
can be explored by boat, or toured
by road. Devenish Island is the
remarkable site of 6th-century
monastic ruins, a Celtic High Cross
and a 30-m (100-ft) Round Tower.

The enchanting Italian Garden at Mount Stewart House

(7) Ulster-American Folk Park

MAP L4 ▪ Near Omagh ▪ 028 9042 8428 ▪ Open Apr–Sep: 10am–5pm Tue–Sun; Oct–Mar: 10am–4pm Tue–Fri, 11am–4pm Sat & Sun ▪ Adm

This fascinating open-air museum reconstructs the lives of Irish emigrants on both sides of the Atlantic, and contains more than 30 historic buildings, churches, settler homesteads and even an emigrant ship.

Period furnishings at Florence Court

(8) Florence Court

MAP L4 ▪ A32, near Enniskillen ▪ 028 6634 8249 ▪ Open hours vary, check website ▪ www.nationaltrust.org

The grandiose 18th-century Palladian Florence Court mansion originally belonged to the Earls of Enniskillen. Among the original features are an ice house and a water-driven sawmill.

(9) Mount Stewart House

MAP L6 ▪ Strangford Lough, near Newtownards ▪ 028 4278 8387 ▪ Lakeside Gardens: open 10am–4:30pm daily; House and Formal Gardens: open mid-Mar–Oct: 11am–5pm daily ▪ Adm

The 18th-century Neo-Classical home of the Marchioness of Londonderry displays a superb art collection, and stands in landscaped gardens with remarkable plant collections. There are exquisite planned views, extraordinary topiary, and many odd stone-carvings representing creatures such as dodos and dinosaurs.

(10) Derry (Londonderry)

MAP K4

At the heart of Derry (Londonderry), is a fascinating walled Plantation town, its 400-year-old fortifications almost intact. Free Derry Corner contains the famous political mural "You Are Now Entering Free Derry", which was painted in 1969.

THE SIX COUNTIES

The nine counties of the Kingdom of Ulster were the last part of Ireland to be subdued by the English. The kingdom's takeover in 1607 led to an exodus of Irish nobility, whose lands were "planted" with British Protestants. When the War of Independence created the Republic of Ireland, six of the Ulster counties remained British under the name of Northern Ireland.

Places to Eat

PRICE CATEGORIES
For a three-course meal for one with
half a bottle of wine (or equivalent
meal), taxes and extra charges.
....
£ under £35 ■ ££ £35–£55 ■ £££ over £55

1 **10 The Port**
MAP L6 ■ The Port Hotel,
The Strand, Portaferry ■ 028 4272
8231 ■ ££
This restaurant on the shores
of Strangford Lough has a high
reputation for top-quality shellfish
and other seafood, most of it fresh
from the waters of the lough.

2 **OX**
MAP L6 ■ 1 Oxford St,
Belfast ■ 028 9031 4121 ■ Closed L;
Sun & Mon ■ £££
Offering a menu that is centred
around local and seasonal produce,
this award-winning restaurant,
overlooking the River Lagan, serves
creative dishes such as hay-baked
beetroot and Skeaghanore duck.

3 **James Street**
MAP L6 ■ 21 James St South,
Belfast ■ 028 9560 0700 ■ £££
Renowned for its beef, which is
cooked over a charcoal grill, this
restaurant has a cool contemporary
vibe, and a fantastic drinks menu.

4 **Mourne Seafood Bar**
MAP L6 ■ 10 Main St, Dundrum,
Newcastle ■ 028 4375 1377 ■ Closed
Mon & Tue ■ ££
Large portions of fresh local
seafood, including shellfish from
the restaurant's own shellfish
beds, are on the menu here.
Steak and chicken dishes are
available too.

5 **Pier 36**
MAP L6 ■ The Parade,
Donaghadee ■ 028 9188 4466 ■ ££
The award-winning Pier 36 on the
quayside serves great seafood, local
game, steaks and sharing platters.

6 **The Morning Star**
MAP L6 ■ 17–19 Pottinger's
Entry, Belfast ■ 028 9023 5986 ■ £
Fine local seafood, meat and poultry
dishes feature at this historic award-
winning gastro-pub.

7 **Deanes EIPIC**
MAP L6 ■ 28–40 Howard St,
Belfast ■ 028 9033 1134 ■ Closed
Sun–Thu L; Fri D ■ £££
Enjoy modern, innovative cuisine
at this Michelin-starred restaurant
with flawless service and set menus.

Outdoor seating at The Bushmills Inn

8 **The Bushmills Inn**
MAP K5 ■ 9 Dunluce Rd,
Bushmills ■ 028 2073 3000 ■ ££
In the village that produces Ulster's
finest whiskey is an atmospheric,
old coaching inn, with open fires
and gas lighting. Try the Antrim
cod or the whiskey-cured salmon.

9 **Walled City Brewery**
MAP K4 ■ 70 Ebrington Sq,
Derry ■ www.walledcitybrewery.com
■ ££
It's not just the beer that brings
the crowds to this cool brewery. The
menu here features hearty pub grub
that always hits the spot.

10 **Crown Liquor Saloon**
MAP L6 ■ 46 Great Victoria St,
Belfast ■ 028 9024 3187 ■ ££
Local favourites are served at this
lovely old pub, such as speciality sau-
sages, chops as well as seasonal pies.

See map on p116
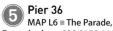

Top 10 Dublin Streetsmart

A popular pub in the lively Temple Bar district, Dublin

Getting Around

Arriving by Air

From more than 20 UK airports, **British Airways** and **Aer Lingus** run regular flights to Dublin and other major Irish cities. Aer Lingus, **Delta**, **Air Canada** and **Air Transat** all fly direct to Dublin from cities across the US and Canada; some also fly to Shannon in the south-west of Ireland. All travellers from Australia and New Zealand have to fly to Dublin via the UK or Europe.

Dublin Airport has two terminals (1 and 2) and is 10 km (6 miles) north of the city centre. From the airport to the city centre, it takes 30–40 minutes using either of the **Dublin Express** buses. Two routes run (numbers 782 and 784), with different drop-off points across the city, and tickets cost €8 (or €12 return). Both depart every 30 minutes from around 4am until around 12:30am. Alternatively, **Aircoach** (route 700) runs 24 hours and costs €7 (€12 return). Tickets for both Aircoach and the Dublin Express can be bought on board. The no. 16 **Dublin Bus** is a cheaper service: a single fare costs €3.30. Taxis are around €30; there is no direct rail link.

Public Transport

Ireland's main transport authorities, **Transport for Ireland** in the Republic of Ireland and **Translink** in Northern Ireland, provide inform-ation on safety and hygiene measures, time-tables, ticket information, transport maps and more on their websites.

Train Travel

Both the Republic of Ireland and Northern Ireland generally have a reliable train network across the country.

DART (Dublin Area Rapid Transit) electric rail serves 30 stations between Malahide north of the centre of Dublin and Greystones to the south, with several stops in Dublin city centre. An all-day ticket allows unlimited travel on all DART trains for €12.15. Multi-day rail and bus tickets are also available. Dublin's light rail service, **Luas**, links the city centre with suburban areas. The Luas lines connect with DART rail at Connolly Station.

The Republic of Ireland's rail network is run by **Irish Rail** (Iarnród Éireann). The journey from Dublin to Belfast takes two hours, with prices from €30 return.

Bus Travel

Dublin Bus offers services from 6am until 11:30pm. Nitelink Buses operate every 30 minutes from midnight to 4am Friday and Saturday from St Stephen's Green, Westmoreland Street, College Green, D'Olier Street and O'Connell Street. Green-and-cream bus stops are for the various Hop-on Hop-off tourist buses. Beyond the city, the coach network is cheaper than train travel. **Bus Éireann's** Open Road pass gives unlimited bus travel on any 3 out of 6 days. Visitors to Dublin, Limerick, Galway, Cork and Waterford can purchase a **Leap Card** which offers discounts on public transport services.

Translink operates throughout Northern Ireland and provides express links between major towns. Timetables and tickets are available at major bus stations.

Taxis

Taxis are plentiful in Dublin, though outside of the city they are rarer. The best places to find them are at train or bus stations, hotels and taxi ranks – your hotel or B&B will also be able to provide details. Taxis are identified by an illuminated sign displaying the driver's licence number on the roof. Four- or eight-seater taxis are available and prices are usually based on metered mileage; if not, it is always best to confirm the fare to your destination before you travel. **Lynk** and **Fonacab** are taxi services in Dublin and Belfast, respectively; they can be booked online or by phone. In both cities, taxis can also be booked via the Uber app.

Driving in Ireland

Driving is perhaps the best way to take in

all that Ireland has to offer. Drivers must carry their passport and insurance documentation if driving their own vehicle. Driving licences issued by any of the EU member states are valid throughout the EU. If visiting from outside the EU, you may need to apply for an International Driving Permit. Check with your local automobile association before you travel.

Roads are well surfaced and are generally in good condition. Many sections have been upgraded to motorways, and there has been extensive construction of two-lane carriageways. For roadside assistance, contact the **AA** or **AA Ireland**.

Cycle Hire

Dublin is extremely bike-friendly, with over 120 miles (193 km) of cycle lanes, many of which are safely separated from road traffic. Outside the city, Ireland's country roads make touring by bicycle a real joy. The unreliable weather, however, can be a hindrance.

Bike rental companies rent bikes to tourists and are usually open six or seven days a week in larger cities. It is often possible to rent a bike in one town and drop it off at another for a charge. You can also take bikes on most trains and some buses, though some request a reservation.

Boats and Ferries

Dublin Port is close to the city centre. Dublin Bus no. 53 connects the port with the city's main bus station and city centre. Nine ports in Great Britain and two in France provide ferry crossings to Ireland's six main ports. Most ferries offer drive-on/drive-off facilities for vehicles. **P&O Ferries** and **Stena Line** run regular domestic ferries and international services to Ireland from the UK and France.

Walking

Dublin is compact enough to explore on foot, and walking is the most agreeable way to take in local life.

Beyond the city, an extensive network of footpaths covers both the Republic of Ireland and Northern Ireland, from coastal trails to routes through mountains. The 1,024 km (636 mile) Ulster Way is the longest trail in Northern Ireland, while the Coast to Coast trail extends 600 kms (370 miles) across the Republic of Ireland.

DIRECTORY

ARRIVING BY AIR

Aer Lingus
W aerlingus.com

Air Canada
W aircanada.com

Aircoach
W aircoach.ie

Airlink
W dublinbus.ie

Air Transat
W airtransat.com

British Airways
W britishairways.com

Delta
W delta.com

Dublin Airport
W dublinairport.com

Dublin Bus
W dublinbus.ie

Dublin Express
W dublinexpress.ie

PUBLIC TRANSPORT

Translink
W translink.co.uk

Transport for Ireland
W transportforireland.ie

TRAIN TRAVEL

DART
W irishrail.ie

Irish Rail
W irishrail.ie

Luas
W luas.ie

BUS TRAVEL

Bus Eireann
W buseireann.ie

Leap Card
W leapcard.ie

TAXI

Fonacab
W fonacab.ie

Lynk
W lynk.com

DRIVING IN IRELAND

AA
W aerlingus.com

AA Ireland
W aerlingus.com

BOATS AND FERRIES

Dublin Port
W dublinport.ie

P&O Ferries
W poferries.com

Stena Line
W stenaline.co.uk

Practical Information

Passports and Visas

For entry requirements, including visas, consult your nearest Irish or British embassy or the **INIS** or **UK Government** websites. From late 2023, citizens of the UK, US, Canada, Australia and New Zealand do not need a visa for stays of up to three months, but must apply in advance for the European Travel Information and Authorization System (**ETIAS**). Visitors from other countries may also require an ETIAS, so check before travelling. EU nationals do not need a visa or an ETIAS.

The border crossing between the Republic and Northern Ireland is normally simple, with few formalities. Following the UK's exit from the EU, the Northern Ireland protocol was put in place to avoid a hard border.

The Embassies of the United Kingdom and the United States are both located in Dublin.

Government Advice

Now more than ever, it is important to consult both your and the Irish or UK's government's advice before travelling. The **UK Foreign, Commonwealth & Development Office (FCDO)**, the **US State Department**, the **Australian Department of Foreign Affairs and Trade** and the **Ireland Department of Foreign Affairs** offer the latest information on security, health and local regulations.

Customs Information

You can find information on the laws relating to goods and currency taken in or out of the Republic of Ireland on the **Tourism Ireland** website. You don't have to pay duty on goods you bring into Ireland if you bought them in another EU country. However, if you exceed certain quantities, you may be asked by customs officials to show that the goods are for your personal use only.

If you're arriving in Ireland from outside the EU, you can bring in certain goods free of duty subject to these limits: 200 cigarettes, 50 cigars or 250g of smoking tobacco; 1 litre of spirits (more than 22%) or 2 litres of fortified wine; 4 litres of wine or 16 litres of beer; 50g of perfume and 250ml of eau de toilette.

Insurance

We recommend that you take out a comprehensive insurance policy covering theft, loss of belongings, medical care, cancellations and delays, and read the small print. EU citizens are eligible for free emergency medical care in the Republic of Ireland provided they have a valid European Health Insurance Card (**EHIC**) or UK Global Health Insurance Card (**GHIC**).

Health

Both the Republic of Ireland and Northern Ireland have very good healthcare systems. Emergency medical care for EU and UK citizens is free of charge for all those that have an EHIC or GHIC. Be sure to present the card as soon as possible. You may have to pay for treatment and reclaim the money later. For non-emergencies and non-EU visitors, payment of medical bills is the patient's responsibility. It is therefore important to arrange comprehensive medical insurance before you travel. In the Republic of Ireland, you may need to pay a fee if you are not referred to the hospital by a GP.

Medical advice and a wide range of medical supplies are available over the counter at Irish pharmacies. Note, however, that some medicines can only be obtained with a doctor's prescription. If you have, or are likely to have, special medical needs it's worth bringing your own treatments, clearly labelled, and a letter from your own doctor giving the generic name of any medication you might require during your stay. There are a good handful of late-night pharmacies: Hickey's Late Night Pharmacy on O'Connell Street in Dublin, for example, is open seven days a week until 10pm.

Smoking, Alcohol and Drugs

A smoking ban is enforced inside all public places, including bars, cafés, restaurants and hotels. The possession of illegal drugs is prohibited and could result in a prison sentence.

The legal limit for drivers in the Republic of Ireland is 50 mg of alcohol per 100 ml of blood and in Northern Ireland it is 80 mg of alcohol per 100 ml of blood. This is roughly equivalent to a small glass of wine or a pint of regular-strength lager.

ID

There is no requirement for visitors to carry ID, but you may occasionally be asked to show your passport. If you don't have it, you may be asked to present the original document within 12 hours.

Personal Security

Ireland is generally a very safe travel destination, though visitors should be wary of street crimes and potential pickpockets in Dublin and other cities

and towns, particularly in central areas after dark.

The **Irish Tourist Assistance Service (ITAS)** provides practical support to victims of crime and can liaise with embassies, organize money transfers and ticket replacements, and cancel credit cards among other services. Main bus and rail stations usually have lost property offices. If you are mugged or attacked, inform the local police, known as the An Garda Siochana (Gardaí for short): its head-quarters are in Phoenix Park in Dublin, and the city-centre station is on Store Street.

For emergency police, fire brigade or ambulance services, call 999. Contact your embassy if you have your passport stolen, or in the event of a serious crime or accident. You must report any stolen property to the police station immediately.

In Northern Ireland during July, visitors may find themselves caught up in slow-moving

traffic behind an Orange march. Tensions between local communities can be higher at this time, leading to a potential increase in criminal activity, but the affected areas should be easily avoided.

As a rule, the Irish are accepting of all people regardless of their race, gender or sexuality. The Republic of Ireland recognized the right to legally change your gender in 2015; this right was granted in 2005 in Northern Ireland. Same-sex marriage was legalized in the Republic in 2015 and in Northern Ireland in 2020.

Some rural areas can be more conservative in their outlook, and some individuals in these areas may be less welcoming, particularly if they are of strong faith. **LGBT Ireland** and **Outhouse** in Dublin offer support for the LGBTQ+ community. Outhouse also run a community centre on Capel Street.

DIRECTORY

PASSPORTS AND VISAS

ETIAS
w etiasvisa.com

INIS
w inis.gov.le

UK Government
w gov.uk

GOVERNMENT ADVICE

Australian Department of Foreign Affairs and Trade
w dfat.gov.au

Ireland Department of Foreign Affairs
w dfa.ie

UK Foreign, Commonwealth & Development Office (FCDO)
w gov.uk/foreign-travel-advice

US Department of State
w travel.state.gov

CUSTOMS INFORMATION

Tourism Ireland
w ireland.com

INSURANCE

EHIC
w ec.europa.eu

GHIC
w nhs.uk/global-health-insurance-card

PERSONAL SECURITY

Emergency Services
C 999

ITAS
w itas.ie

LGBT Ireland
w lgbt.ie

Outhouse Dublin
w outhouse.ie

Travellers with Specific Requirements

Dublin is becoming more accessible for people with specific requirements, and many top attractions are now wheelchair accessible. Most sights and facilities in the city cater to those with visual or hearing impairments, with many museums, including the National Museum of Ireland, welcoming guide dogs. Most government offices and embassies in Dublin provide Irish Sign Language interpreters, and have installed loop counter systems to assist hearing aid users.

All buses and trains in the city provide ramps for ease of access, and larger hotels are required to provide access for wheelchair users. If additional options are required in a hotel, it is recommended that you phone ahead.

Outside of Dublin, wheelchair accesibility on rural buses is generally lacking compared to larger cities. **Accessible Ireland** gives information on accommodation, transport and attractions for those with mobility issues or visual or hearing impairment, while **Disability Action** in Northern Ireland offers an advice service.

Time Zone

Ireland is on Greenwich Mean Time, which is 1 hour behind Continental European Time and 5 hours ahead of US Eastern Standard Time. Time shifts 1 hour ahead to Irish Standard Time in summer (roughly April to October).

Money

The currency in the Republic of Ireland is the euro, with 100 cents to the euro. In Northern Ireland, the currency is the pound. Most shops and restaurants accept major credit and debit cards, while prepaid currency cards and American Express are accepted in some. Contactless payments are accepted by all major retailers, although not on public transport. If travelling beyond large cities, it is worth keeping some cash to hand in case card payment isn't on offer.

Tipping is optional. If you are pleased with the service in a restaurant it is customary to leave a tip of 10 per cent of the total bill. Porters and housekeeping appreciate €1 or £1 per bag.

Electrical Appliances

The electrical supply in Ireland is 230v/50Hz. Plugs are of a three-square-pin type.

Mobile Phones and Wi-Fi

Mobile networks in Ireland use European 3G and 4G standards, and Dublin now benefits from good 5G coverage with some mobile providers. Free Wi-Fi hotspots are available in main towns and cities. Cafés and restaurants usually provide access to Wi-Fi.

Postal Services

Postboxes in Ireland are green, and stamps can be bought from newsagents and post offices. The **General Post Office** in Dublin's O'Connell Street is open from 10am to 5pm Monday to Saturday.

Weather

Ireland is wet and mild all year round, but generally without extremes. It rarely freezes except in the uplands, while summer can see hot spells.

Opening Hours

Many museums close on Sunday mornings. Most shops open from 9am to 6pm Monday to Saturday; Sunday hours are more limited. Banks open from 10am to 4pm Monday to Friday. Pubs are open from 10:30am to 11:30pm Monday to Thursday, 10:30am to 12:30am Friday and Saturday, and noon to 11pm Sunday.

The COVID-19 pandemic proved that situations can change suddenly. Always check before visiting attractions and hospitality venues for up-to-date hours and booking requirements.

Visitor Information

Visitor information centres in Dublin offer a range of services. **Visit Dublin** is the city's main information centre, and the website offers essential itineraries for every season. Hotel lobbies across the city generally have various leaflets for a range of attractions. Other useful websites include **Dublin Town** and **Totally Dublin**. **Fáilte Ireland**, the Irish Tourist Board, and **Discover Northern Ireland**, the Northern Irish Tourist Board, have centres throughout Ireland. **Discover Ireland** has a website with listings of information centres, including an office in the Arrivals Hall at Dublin Airport Terminal 2 (6am to 7pm daily). **Best of Dublin** is an annual magazine with the latest information on the city which is available in print and online.

Local Customs

Visitors should be aware of the tensions between Northern Ireland and the Republic of Ireland and their tumultuous history, though most tourists who remain in Dublin will not experience any trouble. Be respectful of the religious beliefs and political opinions of the local people. Though

Dublin is now a highly diverse modern city, the Republic of Ireland is around 80 per cent Roman Catholic, which means that it may be difficult to find a non-Catholic church outside of the capital.

Language

The Republic of Ireland is officially bilingual, while English is the official language of Northern Ireland. In the Republic, most road signs have place names in both English and Irish. English is the spoken language everywhere apart from a few parts of the far west, called Gaeltachts, but from time to time you may find signs written only in Irish.

Taxes and Refunds

The rate of VAT is 23 per cent in the Republic of Ireland, while in Northern Ireland it is in line with the UK's standard rate of 20 per cent. Non-EU residents are entitled to a tax refund subject

to certain conditions. In order to claim this, request a tax receipt and relevant documentation when you purchase your goods. When leaving the country, present these papers, your receipt and ID at customs to receive your refund.

Accommodation

Dublin offers a variety of accommodation, including luxury five-star hotels, family-run B&Bs and budget hostels catering to tourists of all ages. Lodgings fill up and prices are often inflated in the summer months (from June to September), so it's worth booking in advance to secure the best deal.

A comprehensive list of accommodation across Ireland can be found on Tourism Ireland, Ireland's official tourist website *(p125)*. **Irish Hotels Federation** produces the *Be Our Guest* guide, which is available online or in print. It also earmarks a range of hotels that are wheelchair-friendly.

DIRECTORY

TRAVELLERS WITH SPECIFIC REQUIREMENTS

Accessible Ireland
🔳 accessibleireland.com

Disability Action
🔳 disabilityaction.org

POSTAL SERVICES

General Post Office
🔳 anpost.ie

VISITOR INFORMATION

Best of Dublin
🔳 hotpress.com

Discover Ireland
🔳 discoverireland.ie

Discover Northern Ireland
🔳 discovernorthern ireland.com

Dublin Town
🔳 dublintown.ie

Fáilte Ireland
🔳 failteireland.ie

Totally Dublin
🔳 totallydublin.ie

Visit Dublin
🔳 visitdublin.com

City Sightseeing
🔳 citysightseeing dublin.ie

CityScape
🔳 cityscapetours.ie

Dublin Free Walking Tour
🔳 dublinfreewalking tour.ie

Dublin Pass
🔳 dublinpass.com

ACCOMMODATION

Irish Hotels Federation
🔳 ihf.ie

Places to Stay

PRICE CATEGORIES

For a standard, double room per night (with breakfast if included), taxes and extra charges.

€ under €100   €€ €100–200   €€€ over €200

Luxury Hotels

The Clarence

MAP D4 ▪ 6–8 Wellington Quay, Dublin ▪ 01 407 0800 ▪ www.theclarence. ie ▪ €€€

Once owned by the Irish rock band U2, this refurbished hotel is a design lover's dream, with herringbone floors and modern art aplenty. Located in the buzzing Temple Bar area (see pp22–3) and overlooking the Liffey, it is one of the trendiest places to stay in the city.

The Davenport

MAP G5 ▪ 8–10 Merrion St Lower, Dublin ▪ 01 607 3600 ▪ www.davenport hotel.ie ▪ €€€

Housed in a very beautiful Georgian building, The Davenport has traditional, stylish rooms with modern facilities, and a fine restaurant and bar.

Dylan

MAP T2 ▪ Eastmoreland Place, Dublin ▪ 01 660 3000 ▪ www.dylan.ie ▪ €€€

A luxurious five-star boutique hotel in Ballsbridge, one of Dublin's most affluent areas, Dylan is tucked away just off Baggot Street and within walking distance of all the city's main attractions. The hotel is stylish and charming, has a relaxing restaurant and impeccable service.

The Fitzwilliam

MAP E5 ▪ St Stephen's Green, Dublin ▪ 01 478 7000 ▪ www.fitzwilliam hoteldublin.com ▪ €€€

Designed by the Conran partnership, this award-winning hotel offers luxurious rooms and beautiful views over Stephen's Green.

The K Club

MAP N5 ▪ Straffan, Co Kildare ▪ 01 601 7200 ▪ www.kclub.ie ▪ €€€

Located 30 minutes away from Dublin, this five-star hotel has two championship golf courses; designed by Arnold Palmer, they are considered to be among the finest in Europe.

The Marker

MAP T2 ▪ Grand Canal Sq, Docklands, Dublin ▪ 01 687 5100 ▪ www. themarkerhoteldublin. com ▪ €€€

Dublin's hippest Docklands address makes a bold statement with its checkerboard façade and colour-splashed contemporary interiors. There's an award-winning spa, a rooftop bar and terrace overlooking the city.

The Merrion

MAP G6 ▪ Upper Merrion St, Dublin ▪ 01 603 0600 ▪ www.merrionhotel.com ▪ €€€

One of Dublin's finest hotels, the interiors of The Merrion are an embodiment of Georgian elegance. It has ornate plasterwork, antiques, Irish fabrics, marble bathrooms as well as a two-Michelin-starred restaurant. The modern world hasn't been totally forgotten – there is also a swimming pool, spa, gym and business facilities.

Morrison

MAP D3 ▪ Ormond Quay, Dublin ▪ 01 887 2400 ▪ www.morrison hotel.ie ▪ €€€

Part of the Hilton Group, this boutique hotel is located in Dublin's city centre. Behind the Georgian façade of the Morrison is a chic interior, with its very own private art gallery overlooking a courtyard garden.

The Shelbourne

MAP F6 ▪ 27 St Stephen's Green, Dublin ▪ 01 663 4500 ▪ www.the shelbourne.com ▪ €€€

From the moment you enter the wrought-iron canopied entrance to this beautiful hotel, you will be won over by the grace and charm that have brought loyal customers here since the 19th century.

The Westbury

MAP E5 ▪ Balfe St, Dublin ▪ 01 679 1122 ▪ www. doylecollection.com ▪ €€€

For sheer five-star luxury it's hard to better this classy hotel – the accommodation of choice for politicians and celebrities. It has two fine restaurants and a glamorous cocktail bar. The afternoon tea here is something of an institution.

Mid-range Hotels

Grand Hotel
MAP U1 ■ Grove Rd,
Malahide ■ 01 845 0000
■ www.thegrand.ie ■ €€
Many rooms in this
Malahide hotel have lovely
sea views. There are a
variety of restaurants
and pubs that are located
within walking distance,
and the hotel has a heated
swimming pool, health
centre and gymnasium.

Herbert Park
MAP T2 ■ Ballsbridge,
Dublin ■ 01 667 2200
■ www.herbertparkhotel.
ie ■ €€
A modern hotel, with huge
windows looking out over
lovely parkland. Contem-
porary Irish art decorates
the communal areas,
including the lounge
and the fine restaurant.

Brooks Hotel
MAP E5 ■ Drury St, Dublin
■ 01 670 4000 ■ www.
brookshotel.ie ■ €€€
With its dark-wood foyer
and bar, Brooks exudes
old-world style and ele-
gance. Downstairs, the
restaurant sports a more
modern decor, featuring
locally sourced food. Major
tourist attractions
aroundthe hotel include
Trinity College and Dublin
Castle. The lively pubs
and bars of Grafton Street
are just minutes away.

The Croke Park
MAP T2 ■ Jones's Rd,
Dublin ■ 01 871 4444
■ www.doylecollection.
com ■ €€€
This sophisticated city
hotel is right across the
road from Croke Park
stadium, the heart of Irish
sporting life. It's a real
hub on match days. The
hotel offers shopping and
theatre packages, as well
as one that includes a
tour of the stadium and
the museum.

Jurys Inn Christchurch
MAP D4 ■ Christchurch
Place, Dublin ■ 01 454
0000 ■ www.jurysinns.
com ■ €€€
A popular and comfortable
three-star hotel, Jury's
Inn is a great base for
exploring the heart of
Dublin as it is located
opposite Christ Church,
with Dame Street, Temple
Bar, Trinity College and
Grafton Street all just a
short stroll away. The 182
rooms are all spacious
and smart with en-suite
bathrooms. There is an
on-site bar, a café and a
contemporary restaurant.

Maldron Hotel Smithfield
MAP B2 ■ Smithfield,
Dublin ■ 01 485 0900
■ www.maldronhotel
smithfield.com ■ €€
Set in an excellent
location overlooking
Smithfield Square, this
smart hotel has comfort-
able, modern rooms. It
represents really great
value in an excellent
location. The local pub,
The Cobblestone, is a
classic, and there's an
arthouse cinema next door.

The Morgan
MAP E3 ■ 10 Fleet St,
Temple Bar, Dublin ■ 01
643 7000 ■ www.the
morgan.com ■ €€
With its minimalist, yet
cosy decor of white fab-
rics, beech-wood furniture
and pale walls, the Morgan
encapsulates the contem-
porary style of the Temple
Bar area. In the evenings,
it can be noisy on the
streets, so it's best to
request for a top-floor
room if you possibly can.

The Schoolhouse
MAP T2 ■ Northumberland
Rd, Ballsbridge, Dublin
■ 01 667 5014 ■ www.
schoolhousehotel.com
■ €€
An extraordinary
four-star hotel converted
from a 19th-century
schoolhouse, it saw some
action during the Easter
Rising (see p39). Many
original features have
been retained and former
classrooms have been
converted into a lovely,
atmospheric restaurant
and bar – fortunately, the
modern Irish cuisine is
rather better than your
average school dinner.

The Spencer Hotel
MAP H3 ■ Excise Walk,
IFSC, Dublin ■ 01 433
8800 ■ www.thespencer
hotel.com ■ €€€
The Spencer enjoys a
perfect central location, a
short walk from O'Connell
Street and Trinity College.
The modern, stylish rooms
have floor-to-ceiling windows. You can relax in the
heated pool before enjoy-
ing some Asian-fusion
cuisine or a cocktail-mak-
ing class in the hotel bar.

Riu Plaza The Gresham
MAP E2 ■ 23 Upper
O'Connell St, Dublin ■ 01
874 6881 ■ www.gresham-
hotels-dublin.com ■ €€€
Conveniently located
on the O'Connell Street
(see p70), Dublin's oldest
hotel, now part of Riu
Hotels, sports stunning
Waterford crystal chan-
deliers which add more
than a touch of elegance.

Trinity City Hotel

MAP F4 ■ Pearse St, Dublin ■ 01 648 1000 ■ www.trinitycityhotel. com ■ €€

Overlooking the walls of Trinity College, this hotel has paid attention to every detail, combining Art Deco influences with a modern twist. Most striking are its oversized lilac sofas in the foyer, and the great selection of sculptures.

Townhouse Hotels

Ariel House

MAP T2 ■ 50–54 Lansdowne Rd, Ballsbridge, Dublin ■ 01 668 5512 ■ www.ariel-house.net ■ €€

Stately elegance and charming service are on offer at this Victorian house in a suburb, close to the city centre. It serves excellent afternoon tea. The 37 bedrooms are all en suite and decorated with antique period furniture and pretty fabrics.

Harrington Hall

MAP E6 ■ 70 Harcourt St ■ 01 475 3497 ■ www. harringtonhall.com ■ €€

A collection of Georgian houses have been combined to provide 28 meticulously decorated rooms. The Irish breakfast is an excellent start to a day of sightseeing, and there is a private car park behind the hotel.

Hotel St George

MAP E1 ■ 7 Parnell Sq, Dublin ■ 01 874 5611 ■ www.hotelstgeorge dublin.com ■ €€

The period staircase in this converted Georgian house is one of its most striking features, as well as the crystal chandeliers made from renowned Waterford crystal (see p87). The hotel is conveniently situated for all the attractions north of the Liffey, such as the Hugh Lane Gallery (see p70).

The Mont

MAP G5 ■ 1–4 Merrion St Lower ■ 01 607 3800 ■ www.themonthotel.ie ■ €€

This is one of Dublin's most modish hotels with a Georgian façade. It has 96 quirky designer bedrooms with smart TVs, a trendy bar serving an impressive number of gins and craft beers, a high-tech gym, and a woodfire oven pizza restaurant. It is close to Trinity College, the National Gallery and the main shopping areas.

Pembroke Townhouse

MAP T2 ■ 90 Pembroke Rd, Dublin ■ 01 660 0277 ■ www.pembroketown house.ie ■ €€

The 48 cosy en-suite bedrooms in this townhouse hotel, comprising of three Georgian houses, are fully equipped with modern amenities. A traditional Irish breakfast is offered in the sunny dining room and there is a comfortable lounge.

Roxford Lodge Hotel

MAP T2 ■ 46 Northumberland Rd, Ballsbridge, Dublin ■ 01 668 8572 ■ www.rox fordlodge.ie ■ €€

This elegant Victorian townhouse retains many charming original features. All the rooms are en suite and it is only a short stroll from the city centre.

Waterloo Lodge

MAP T2 ■ 23 Waterloo Rd, Ballsbridge, Dublin ■ 01 668 5380 ■ www. waterloolodge.com ■ €€

There are 19 en-suite bedrooms (including several family rooms) in this Georgian townhouse, which stands in the heart of one of Dublin's most affluent suburbs. The city centre and the Aviva stadium are within walking distance. The lodge also offers free parking, Wi-Fi and a complimentary breakfast.

Baggot Court

MAP G6 ■ 92 Lower Baggot St, Dublin ■ 01 661 2819 ■ www.baggot court.com ■ €€€

Located near St Stephen's Green and the shopping hub of the city on Grafton Street, this converted Georgian townhouse makes an affordable place to stay. The price includes a full Irish or Continental breakfast.

Fitzwilliam Townhouse

MAP G6 ■ 41 Upper Fitzwilliam St, Dublin ■ 01 662 5155 ■ www.fitzwill iamtownhouse.com ■ €€€

In the heart of Georgian Dublin, near St Stephen's Green, this townhouse, with 13 comfortable en-suite rooms, oozes charm. It serves a good breakfast, with cheeses and homemade jams on offer.

Trinity Lodge

MAP F5 ■ 12 South Frederick St, Dublin ■ 01 617 0900 ■ www. trinitylodge.com ■ €€€

The 26 rooms of this Georgian townhouse are all fully equipped, and contemporary in style.

Guesthouses

Windsor Lodge
MAP N6 ▪ 3 Islington Ave, Sandycove, Co Dublin ▪ 01 284 6952 ▪ www.windsorlodge.ie ▪ €
A haven from the bustle of the city, this striking Victorian home is a short stroll from the DART and Dun Laoghaire with its many shops and restaurants.

Albany House
MAP E6 ▪ 84 Harcourt St, Dublin ▪ 01 475 1092 ▪ www.albanyhousedublin.com ▪ €€
This 18th-century house was once owned by the Earl of Clonmel, and is now a characterful and comfortable hotel, blending period furnishings with modern amenities.

Donnybrook Hall
MAP T2 ▪ 6 Belmont Ave, Donnybrook, Dublin ▪ 01 269 1633 ▪ www.donnybrookhall.com ▪ €€
Situated in the leafy area of Donnybrook, just south of the city, this four-star family-run guesthouse is close to many of Dublin's best pubs and restaurants. All of its rooms are en suite and there are several quiet garden rooms and a comfortable sitting room.

Morehampton Townhouse
MAP F2 ▪ 78 Morehampton Rd, Dublin ▪ 01 668 8866 ▪ www.morehamptontownhouse.com ▪ €€
Excellent value for money, this guesthouse is located in leafy Donnybrook, about a 30-minute walk from the city centre. Its single rooms are great for solo travellers.

Kilronan House
MAP T2 ▪ 70 Adelaide Rd, Dublin ▪ 01 475 5266 ▪ www.kilronanhouse.com ▪ €€
Located in a glorious, leafy part of the city, this lovely, old-fashioned guesthouse is a short walk from St Stephen's Green and the National Concert Hall.

King Sitric
MAP U2 ▪ East Pier, Howth, Co Dublin ▪ 01 832 5235 ▪ www.kingsitric.ie ▪ €€
Well known for its seafood restaurant, King Sitric offers excellent accommodation, with eight beautiful rooms overlooking the sea, all named after local lighthouses. Enjoy the bustle of Dublin by day, then return to this haven of seaside calm.

Portmarnock Hotel and Golf Links
MAP U1 ▪ Strand Rd, Portmarnock ▪ 01 846 0611 ▪ www.portmarnock.com ▪ €€
Nestled between a sandy beach and a golf course, this lovely seaside hotel just north of Dublin city is set in the original home of the famous Jameson whiskey family. Needless to say, the bar here has an extensive whiskey list.

Aberdeen Lodge
MAP T2 ▪ 53–55 Park Ave, Ballsbridge, Dublin ▪ 01 283 8155 ▪ www.aberdeen-lodge.com ▪ €€€
A friendly, plush boutique hotel on a tree-lined avenue in Ballsbridge, Aberdeen Lodge has 16 en-suite rooms and serves delicious breakfasts and offers a wonderfully refined setting for a relaxing stay.

Number 31
MAP T2 ▪ 31 Leeson Close, Dublin ▪ 01 676 5011 ▪ www.number31.ie ▪ €€€
This unique hotel, with 21 guest rooms, comprises of two coach houses (converted by Irish architect Sam Stephenson in 1958), connected by private gardens to a classic Georgian house.

Waterloo House
MAP T2 ▪ 8–10 Waterloo Rd, Ballsbridge, Dublin ▪ 01 660 1888 ▪ www.waterloohouse.ie ▪ €€
This family-run, four-star Georgian guesthouse offers 19 fully equipped bedrooms. It also benefits from a private car park.

Waterford, Wicklow, Kilkenny and Limerick Hotels

Butler House
MAP P4 ▪ 15–16 Patrick St, Kilkenny ▪ 056 772 2828 ▪ www.butler.ie ▪ €€
An elegant place to stay in Kilkenny, this Georgian townhouse is near the river and the castle. Rooms are spacious, and staircases lead to the gardens.

Clayton Hotel Limerick
MAP P3 ▪ Steamboat Quay, Limerick ▪ 061 444 100 ▪ www.claytonhotellimerick.com ▪ €€
This 17-storey, landmark hotel in Limerick is right on the waterfront and has great views over the Shannon. Its four-star facilities include a leisure club with swimming pool, sauna and steam room.

For a key to hotel price categories see p128

Dunbrody Country House

MAP Q5 ▪ Arthurstown, Co Wexford ▪ 051 389 600 ▪ www.dunbrody house.com ▪ €€€

Located on the Hook Peninsula, this beautiful country house offers impeccable service, a luxury spa, food prepared by one of Ireland's finest chefs (see p89) and a sprawling parkland.

Hanora's Cottage

MAP Q4 ▪ Nire Valley, Ballymacarbry, Co Waterford ▪ 052 613 6134 ▪ www.hanoras cottage.com ▪ €€

The walking trails on the beautiful Comeragh Mountains near Hanora's Cottage are perfect for working up an appetite for some tasty Irish cuisine in the hotel restaurant, which also has a great vegetarian menu.

Hunter's Hotel

MAP N5 ▪ Newrath Bridge, Rathnew, Co Wicklow ▪ 0404 40106 ▪ www.hunters.ie ▪ €€

There are two acres of pretty gardens at this old coaching inn. Beaches are nearby and the restaurant takes advantage of the fresh fish for its dishes. Ireland's best golf courses are also within easy reach.

Pembroke Kilkenny

MAP P4 ▪ 11 Patrick St, Kilkenny ▪ 056 778 3500 ▪ www.kilkennypembroke hotel.com ▪ €€

Converted from a 1930s racing-car garage, this hotel is right in the heart of Kilkenny. Rooms come with super-king beds and there is live music in the bar every Friday and Saturday night.

Richmond House

MAP Q4 ▪ Cappoquin, Co Waterford ▪ 058 542 78 ▪ www.richmond countryhouse.ie ▪ €€

This 18th-century Georgian country house offers an award-winning restaurant and stunning grounds. Log fires warm period-feature rooms.

Adare Manor

MAP P3 ▪ Main St, Adare Village, Co Limerick ▪ 061 605 200 ▪ www. adaremanor.com ▪ €€€

Perched on the bank of the river Maigue in one of Ireland's prettiest villages, this 19th-century manor house is a five-star luxury hotel. Once the seat of the Earls of Dunraven, it is American-owned. The vast estate features a Tom Fazio championship golf course.

Mount Juliet Estate

MAP P5 ▪ Thomastown, Co Kilkenny ▪ 056 777 3000 ▪ www.mountjuliet. ie ▪ €€€

An 18-hole golf course designed by Jack Nicklaus is at the heart of this 1,500-acre (6-sq-km) estate. It periodically hosts the WGC American Express Championship. The rooms are stunning and it has two award-winning restaurants. There is also a spa and facilities for horse-riding.

Waterford Castle

MAP Q5 ▪ The Island, Waterford ▪ 051 878 203 ▪ www.waterford castleresort.com ▪ €€€

Offering one of the unique hotel experiences in the world, this 15th-century castle is set on a sprawling island overlooking the River Suir. Access is by car ferry only and the hotel is luxuriously furnished with antiques and open fireplaces.

Galway and Connemara Hotels

Foyle's Hotel

MAP M1 ▪ Main St, Clifden, Connemara, Co Galway ▪ 095 21801 ▪ Closed Jan ▪ www. foyleshotel.com ▪ €

A lovely Victorian-era hotel that offers good, old-fashioned comfort and charm, it has been in the Foyle family for nearly a century. The smooth service and idyllic location add to the charm. The attached Marconi restaurant is popular and the breakfast is good.

Ardagh Hotel

MAP M1 ▪ Clifden, Co Galway ▪ 095 21384 ▪ Open Easter–Oct ▪ www.ardaghhotel. com ▪ €€

Located in beautiful Ardbear bay, this three-star hotel has 17 rooms, each with a private bathroom. If long walks amid Connemara's coastal scenery don't draw you here, the award-winning restaurant should.

Cashel House

MAP N2 ▪ Cashel, Co Galway ▪ 095 31001 ▪ www.cashelhouse.ie ▪ €€

An oasis of calm in the Atlantic coast, this hotel rests amid beautiful gardens. Rooms look out onto the gardens or the sea. Antiques and period paintings abound, as do open turf fires. There's a private beach ideal for walks, cycling, horse riding and fishing.

Currarevagh House
MAP N2 ■ Oughterard, Connemara, Co Galway ■ 091 552 312 ■ Open Apr–Nov ■ www.currarevagh.com ■ €€

This country mansion, dating from 1842, is situated right beside Lough Corrib in private woodland. Absorb the splendid isolation of its location by walking in the woods, or take a fishing boat out on the lake before settling down to the popular afternoon tea in the drawing room. The house has 9 bedrooms and its own tennis courts.

Jurys Inn Galway
MAP N3 ■ Quay St, Galway ■ 091 566 444 ■ www.jurysinns.com ■ €€

The Jurys chain offers good value, well-located accommodation. This branch is beside the historic Spanish Arch overlooking Galway Bay.

Ashford Castle
MAP M2 ■ Cong, Co Mayo ■ 094 954 6003 ■ www.ashfordcastle.com ■ €€€

Facilities include a health club with a steam room and a sauna at this glorious five-star hotel and resort set in a castle. Activities at the resort include golf, horse riding, falconry, cruising and fishing on Lough Corrib.

Ballynahinch Castle
MAP N2 ■ Ballynahinch, Recess, Connemara, Co Galway ■ 095 31006 ■ www.ballynahinch-castle.com ■ €€€

Once home to the pirate queen Grace O'Malley (see p110), this casually elegant four-star hotel, set in a huge private estate, enjoys a breath-taking location, ringed by the impressive Twelve Bens Mountains. The award-winning restaurant serves fresh, excellent game and fish.

Delphi Lodge
MAP M2 ■ Leenane, Co Galway ■ 095 42222 ■ www.delphilodge.ie ■ €€€

One of Ireland's most famous fishing lodges, the atmosphere here is elegant, with a library, a billiards room and a large drawing room overlooking the lake. Five restored cottages provide further accommodation. The surroundings are home to abundant wildlife, including falcons, badgers and otters. Fly-fishing for salmon can be done here.

House Hotel
MAP N3 ■ Spanish Parade, Galway ■ 091 538 900 ■ www.thehousehotel.ie ■ €€€

In the thudding heart of Galway's Latin Quarter, with its buskers and bou-tiques, this buzzy place fits in perfectly – set in a converted warehouse and home to the city's top cocktail bar as well as some of its smart bedrooms. The afternoon teas are also superb.

The Twelve Hotel
MAP N2 ■ Barna Village, Galway ■ 091 597 000 ■ www.thetwelvehotel.ie ■ €€€

This award-winning four-star boutique hotel located near the beach is nestled in the sleepy village of Barna. The luxuriously appointed rooms are individually designed, and there is a pizza kitchen and an excel-lent restaurant on site.

Cork and Kerry Hotels

Aherne's Townhouse
MAP Q4 ■ 163 N Main St, Youghal, Co Cork ■ 024 92424 ■ www.ahernes.net ■ €€

This family-run pub is also a hotel-restaurant. The cosy sitting room has an open fireplace and lots of books. Some rooms have balconies.

The Brehon
MAP Q2 ■ Muckross Road, Killarney ■ 064 663 0700 ■ www.thebrehon.com ■ €€

With a piano plinking quietly in the lobby, a full-service Angsana spa and wide-ranging views of the rugged Killarney country-side, The Brehon is the perfect place to get away from the busy life. It also wins rave reviews for its terrific food, which is served in both the fine-dining restaurant and the more informal bar area.

Castlewood House
MAP Q1 ■ The Wood, Dingle, Co Kerry ■ 066 915 2788 ■ www.castlewooddingle.com ■ €€

Many rooms offer a stunning view out onto the bay at this luxury guesthouse. Breakfast is hearty and rooms are spacious and stylish, some with jacuzzi tubs. There's a lounge with DVDs and board games. Hosts Helen and Brian are warm and gracious and ensure guests have a comfortable stay.

For a key to hotel price categories see p128

The Old Bank House

MAP Q3 ■ 10–11 Pearse St, Kinsale, Co Cork ■ 021 477 4075 ■ www.oldbank housekinsale.com ■ €€

Set in two handsome Georgian townhouses facing Kinsale's bustling harbour, this hotel has been voted one of the "Top 100 places to stay in Ireland" every year since 1990. Breakfast, served in the hotel's boutique coffee shop, is excellent.

Shelburne Lodge

MAP Q2 ■ Killowen, Cork Rd, Kenmare, Co Kerry ■ 064 664 1013 ■ Closed Dec–Easter ■ www.shelburnelodge. com ■ €€

Once the home of Lord Shelburne (1737–1805), former prime minister of Great Britain, this beautiful and welcoming guesthouse has roaring log fires and charming, wooden-floored rooms, each furnished with antiques. The house is set in lovely secluded gardens, just a short stroll from the centre of the town.

Ballymaloe House

MAP Q3 ■ Shanagarry, Midleton, Co Cork ■ 021 465 2531 ■ Closed 25 Dec & Jan ■ www.ballymaloe. ie ■ €€€

This ivy-covered Georgian guesthouse on a sprawling 400-acre (2-sq-km) farm is exceptional. Try your hand at golf or tennis, or splash around in the pool before settling down for a pre-dinner drink in the drawing room. The award-winning restaurant serves wholesome traditional food prepared with fresh, local ingredients.

Muckross Park Hotel

MAP Q2 ■ Muckross Village, Killarney, Co Kerry ■ 064 662 3400 ■ www.muckrosspark. com ■ €€€

Located in the heart of Killarney National Park, this Victorian hotel has stunning views across the Lough Leane and Muckross Lake. It is home to the award winning Spa at Muckross. A true retreat, with staff who go out of their way to make your stay as enjoyable as possible, and sublime food in the Yew Tree restaurant.

The Park Hotel

MAP Q2 ■ Kenmare, Co Kerry ■ 064 664 1200 ■ www.parkken mare.com ■ €€€

Set in a fine 19th-century limestone building, this hotel overlooks stunning gardens and Kenmare Bay. Enjoy the restaurant's mix of classic and inventive cooking, relax in the spa or play a round of golf in the adjacent 18-hole course; salmon fishing and horse riding are also available nearby.

The River Lee

MAP Q3 ■ Western Rd, The Lough, Cork ■ 021 425 2700 ■ www.doyle collection.com ■ €€€

This landmark place makes quite a splash on the Cork riverside, with its glass façade and slick dining terrace. Floor-to-ceiling windows enliven the muted ochres and browns – especially if you opt for a fifth-floor room overlooking the water. There's also an excellent spa as well as an indoor pool and fitness centre.

Sheen Falls Lodge

MAP Q2 ■ Kenmare, Co Kerry ■ 064 664 1600 ■ www.sheenfalls lodge.ie ■ €€€

This rambling lodge, situated on a dramatic estate above Sheen Falls and Kenmare Bay, is a relaxing retreat set in picturesque surroundings. The renowned restaurant, La Cascade, overlooks a waterfall. Facilities include a fitness centre, swimming pool and wine cellar.

Northwest and Northern Hotels

Bullitt

MAP L6 ■ 40 Church Lane, Belfast ■ 028 9590 0600 ■ www.bullitthotel. com ■ €

Right in the city centre, the super-hip Bullitt, named after the 1968 Steve McQueen film, offers small but comfortable rooms with lots of personality, including movie-montage art, cool lighting, and "Grub to Go" breakfast bags. There's a sleek courtyard beer garden specializing in craft brews, and a great grill-house restaurant, Taylor & Clay.

Coopershill

MAP L3 ■ Riverstown, Co Sligo ■ 071 916 5108 ■ Closed Nov–Mar ■ www. coopershill.com ■ €€

Set on a sprawling estate of farm and woodland, this 1774 Georgian mansion owned and managed by the O'Hara family is an elegant retreat. Enjoy candlelit dinners served on the family silver, sip drinks by the open log fires and look out for peacocks as you stroll through the beautiful grounds. Try the award-winning venison at the site.

The Cuan

MAP L6 ▪ The Sq, Strangford, Downpatrick ▪ 028 4488 1222 ▪ www. thecuan.com ▪ €€
Beside the square in picturesque Strangford, this welcoming guesthouse could style itself as a restaurant-with-rooms, such is the reputation of owner Peter McErlean's cooking. His seafood chowder is near legendary, and you can work off the calories with some walking, cycling or canoeing at nearby Castle Ward.

Hastings Everglades

MAP K4 ▪ Prehen Rd, Co Derry ▪ 028 7132 1066 ▪ www.hastings hotels.com ▪ €€
This luxurious hotel is in an ideal location next to the River Foyle and beside the 17th-century walled City of Derry. It's a great base for exploring the town or for venturing further afield into the Sperrin Mountains and County Donegal. Spend your evenings relaxing in the huge lounge bar or dining in the restaurant.

Radisson Blu Hotel & Spa

MAP L3 ▪ Balincar, Rosses Point, Sligo ▪ 071 9140 008 ▪ www. radissonhotels.com ▪ €€
Offering lovely views of Sligo Bay and the surrounding mountains, this comfortable hotel is a short drive from Sligo city centre. It features 132 rooms with modern decor as well as a restaurant, bar,

leisure club and spa with pool, Jacuzzi, sauna and steam room.

Rathmullan Country House

MAP K4 ▪ Rathmullan, Co Donegal ▪ 074 915 8188 ▪ www.rathmullan house.com ▪ €€
Located on the shores of Donegal, this hotel has award-winning gardens that lead onto a long sandy beach. Rooms are decorated in period style and family rooms and suites are available. There are also an indoor swimming pool, steam room and tennis courts.

Tara Hotel

MAP L3 ▪ Main St, Killybegs, Co Donegal ▪ 074 974 1700 ▪ www. tarahotel.ie ▪ €€
Located above the harbour in the Donegal fishing port of Killybegs, Tara Hotel is known for its smiling staff and hearty breakfasts; ask for a balcony room and watch the trawlers come and go. The Slieve League cliffs, Europe's highest sea cliffs, are very nearby.

Temple House

MAP M3 ▪ Ballymote, Co Sligo ▪ 087 997 6045 ▪ www.templehouse.ie ▪ €€€
The Perceval family have owned this lovely Georgian country manor house set in vast grounds since 1665; the current building was refurbished in 1864. Rooms have a traditional atmosphere with log fires and canopied beds. The surrouding area has many archaeological sights and the hotel can advise on best spots for walks.

Whitepark House

MAP K5 ▪ 50 Whitepark Rd, Ballintoy, Co Antrim ▪ 028 2073 1482 ▪ www. whiteparkhouse.com ▪ €€
Owner Bob Isles made headlines in 2003 when he became the first man ever to win the AA's "Landlady of the Year" crown. He still offers impeccable bed-and-breakfast at this atmospheric 18th-century house with a garden behind Whitepark Bay. It makes a marvellous base for the Giant's Causeway and Carrick-a-Rede rope bridge.

Bushmills Inn

MAP K5 ▪ 9 Dunluce Rd, Bushmills, Co Antrim ▪ 028 2073 3000 ▪ www.bush millsinn.com ▪ €€€
Once you check into this old coaching inn and mill house, you may find it difficult to leave. Not only will the open peat fires and gas lights make you want to stay, the nearby Bushmills distillery – the oldest in Northern Ireland – may make you forget how to get home.

Hilton Park

MAP L5 ▪ Clones, Co Monaghan ▪ 047 56007 ▪ www.hilton park.ie ▪ €€€
The Madden family have been residing in this grand house since 1734, and have been welcoming guests ever since then. The dining room is sumptuous beyond words, and the six bedrooms are superb, with breathtaking views of the woodlands, gardens and lakes.

For a key to hotel price categories see p128

General Index

Acknowledgments

This edition updated by

Contributor Nicola Brady
Senior Editor Alison McGill
Senior Art Editor Vinita Venugopal
Project Editor Parnika Bagla
Editors Alex Pathe, Anuroop Sanwalia
Assistant Art Editor Divyanshi Shreyaskar
Picture Research Administrator Vagisha Pushp
Manager Picture Research Taiyaba Khatoon
Publishing Assistant Halima Mohammed
Jacket Designer Jordan Lambley
Senior Cartographer Subhashree Bharati
Cartography Manager Suresh Kumar
Senior DTP Designer Tanveer Zaidi
Senior Production Editor Jason Little
Production Controller Kariss Ainsworth
Deputy Managing Editor Beverly Smart
Managing Editors Shikha Kulkarni, Hollie Teague
Managing Art Editor Sarah Snelling
Senior Managing Art Editor Priyanka Thakur
Art Director Maxine Pedliham
Publishing Director Georgina Dee

DK would like to thank the following for their contribution to the previous editions: Hilary Bird, Joe Cornish, Kathryn Glendenning, Therese McKenna, Polly Phillimore, Rough Guides / Mark Thomas, Alan Williams, Andrew Sanger

The publisher would like to thank the following for their kind permission to reproduce their photographs:

Single Sailboat (1874) by Claude Monet 17tl; The Cottage Girl (1785) by Thomas Gainsborough 17bc.
The Olympia Theatre: Dara Munnis 48t.
Patrick Guilbaud: 67c
Pichet Restaurant: Paul McCarthy 2tr, 36-7, 53t, 67br.
Powerscourt Estate: 75b.
Project Arts Centre: Butterflies and Bones as part of The Casement Project by Project Artist Fearghus O Ó Conchu úir, Photo by Stephen Wright 22bl.
Robert Harding Picture Library: Roy Rainford 106tr; Hugh Rooney 40tl; Peter Zoeller 42tc.
Shutterstock.com: Ross Mahon 69tl; trabantos 34-35ca
Smock Alley Theatre: 49cl.
SuperStock: imageBROKER 51tl, The Irish Image Collection 61cr.
Taste At Rustic: Ten20photography / Damian Bligh 52cl.
The Bushmills Inn: Kris Dickson 119cr.
The National Maritime Museum of Ireland: 74cra.
The Winding Stair: Dave Sweeney 73cra.
© Trustees of the Chester Beatty, Dublin: 20tl, 20bl, 21t, 21bl.
Viking Splash Tours: 46-7b.
Whelan's Bar: Dara Munnis 51br.
The Wyatt Hotel: 111r.

Cover
Front and spine: **4Corners:** Maurizio Rellini.
Back: **4Corners:** Maurizio Rellini b; **Alamy Stock Photo:** Keith Poynton tr, Simon Reddy tl; **iStockphoto.com:** jamegaw crb, SAKhanPhotography tr; **Robert Harding Picture Library:** ProCip cla.

Pull Out Map Cover
4Corners: Maurizio Rellini.

All other images © Dorling Kindersley For further information see: www.dkimages.com

Illustrator Chris Orr & Associates
chrisorr.com

Penguin
Random
House

First Edition 2003

Published in Great Britain by
Dorling Kindersley Limited
DK, One Embassy Gardens, 8 Viaduct Gardens, London SW11 7BW, UK

The authorised representative in the EEA is Dorling Kindersley Verlag GmbH. Arnulfstr. 124, 80636 Munich, Germany

Published in the United States by
DK Publishing, 1745 Broadway, 20th Floor, New York, NY 10019, USA

Copyright © 2003, 2023 Dorling
Kindersley Limited

A Penguin Random House Company

23 24 25 26 10 9 8 7 6 5 4 3 2 1

A CIP catalogue record is available
from the British Library.

A catalogue record for this book is available from the Library of Congress.

ISSN 1479-344X
ISBN 978-0-2416-1584-3

Printed and bound in Malaysia

www.dk.com

As a guide to abbreviations in visitor information blocks: ***Adm*** *= admission charge;* ***L*** *= lunch;* ***D*** *= dinner.*

This book was made with Forest Stewardship Council™ certified paper – one small step in DK's commitment to a sustainable future.
**For more information go to
www.dk.com/our-green-pledge**

Selected Ireland Map Index